Diabetes
COOKBOOK

54
— 60
66
76

American Medical Association

Diabetes
COOKBOOK

RECIPES
Maureen Callahan, R.D.
Karen A. Levin

PHOTOGRAPHS
Jim Franco
Sheri Giblin

MEREDITH® BOOKS
Des Moines, Iowa

CONTENTS

LIVING WELL WITH DIABETES

EATING IS ONE OF LIFE'S GREATEST PLEASURES, AND EATING WELL IS ONE OF THE MOST IMPORTANT THINGS YOU CAN DO FOR YOUR HEALTH. EVERY DAY, RESEARCHERS DISCOVER A NEW LINK BETWEEN DIET AND HEALTH. If you are one of the millions of Americans who have diabetes, choosing the right foods may sometimes seem like a chore. Although it's true that if you have diabetes you need to carefully balance the food you eat with your physical activity to keep your blood glucose at a healthy level, eating does not have to be a burden. With only a small amount of planning and preparation and the delicious recipes you'll find in this cookbook, you can eat just as well as anyone else and enjoy food just as much.

The American Medical Association has developed this diverse collection of recipes with you in mind, whether you have diabetes or have been warned that you're at risk of developing it—or whether you simply want to eat more healthfully. The sixty dishes in this book are not only tasty, but also attractive and quick and easy to prepare. They're designed by nutrition professionals to help you stay in good health while making everyday eating a pleasurable part of life for you and your family.

UNDERSTANDING DIABETES

If you have diabetes, your doctor and diabetes educator or dietitian have helped you develop a nutrition plan. If you have been told your blood sugar level puts you at risk of developing diabetes, your doctor has no doubt recommended steps you can take to reduce this risk. It pays, however, to remember the facts about the two main forms of diabetes.

CONTROL YOUR BLOOD SUGAR

Keeping your blood sugar level in the range your doctor has set for you can help you prevent or slow complications from diabetes. Here are some helpful tips:

• Eat about the same amount of food every day.

• Eat meals and snacks at about the same time each day.

• Don't skip meals or snacks.

• Take your diabetes medicine at the same time every day.

• Try to exercise at about the same time each day.

Disease-fighting foods (facing page, clockwise from top left): white beans, high in fiber and protein; arugula, a flavorful green high in antioxidants; salmon, a source of heart-healthy omega-3 fatty acids; and a salad with vitamin-rich spinach and beets.

Type 1 diabetes

Type 1 diabetes usually develops during childhood when the pancreas stops producing insulin or doesn't produce it in sufficient quantity, causing sugar to build up in the blood. Type 1 diabetes is much less common than type 2; only about 5 to 10 percent of people with diabetes have this form. To stay healthy, people with type 1 diabetes must follow a carefully controlled diet and have daily injections of insulin throughout life to keep their blood sugar level in a normal range.

Type 2 diabetes

Of the 17 million Americans with diabetes, 90 to 95 percent have type 2, which is becoming epidemic throughout the world and striking increasing numbers of children.

Type 2 diabetes develops from an interaction of genes and lifestyle factors, especially lack of exercise and excess weight, which cause the body to stop responding to the effects of insulin, a hormone that enables the body to use sugar for energy.

Unlike type 1 diabetes, type 2 diabetes can sometimes be prevented and controlled with measures such as regular exercise and weight loss.

Blood sugar's role

Sugar is the fuel that energizes all the cells of the body, but excess sugar in the blood makes some components of the blood "sticky" and the blood vessels more likely to develop fatty deposits that can build up and reduce or block blood flow. The damage to blood vessels and nerves from excess sugar in the blood over time can lead to serious long-term complications including vision loss, kidney disease, stroke from high blood pressure, and heart disease.

People who have precise control of their blood sugar are much less likely to experience these complications— all the more reason to consistently follow the recommendations of your doctor and diabetes educator.

MANAGING YOUR DIABETES

Your blood sugar level depends on factors such as your diet, weight, activity, and medications—even your emotions. If you have type 1 diabetes, you will probably be most concerned about balancing your food intake with your insulin dosages and exercise. If you have type 2, you may be more interested in weight control.

Low-fat dishes such as Pork Loin with Apples (page 74) fit well in diabetic diets if balanced with whole grains, beans, and greens.

Biking and walking (facing page) are simple activities that can help people with diabetes control their blood sugar and weight.

Watch your diet

Diet is a major factor in controlling blood sugar levels, but there is no standard diabetic diet that works for everyone.

What diabetic meal plans have in common is that they are based on scientific understanding of the nutrient needs of the human body. They are heart-healthy, calorie-conscious, high in fiber and other important nutrients, and low in harmful fats and sweets. Specifically, they are rich in whole grains, vegetables, legumes, and fruits, and they replace unhealthy fats (such as those in fatty meats) with healthy plant-based fats (such as olive oil) and omega-3 fatty acids (from fish).

Work with your doctor or dietitian to develop a personal nutrition plan designed to provide essential nutrients and help you maintain a healthy weight. The recipes in this book can be part of your plan, helping you control your blood sugar levels while you enjoy satifying meals.

Stay at a healthy weight

Obesity, which is widespread in the United States and increasing, is one of the major factors contributing to the epidemic of type 2 diabetes. Losing weight can help you prevent type 2 diabetes or, if you already have diabetes, can reduce the severity of the disease by making your body more sensitive to insulin. Even a moderate weight loss—10 pounds or so—can reduce your blood sugar and benefit your health.

No miracle diet exists: to lose weight and keep the weight off, you have to consume fewer calories than your body burns. Avoid diets that claim otherwise.

Because managing your diabetes with drugs or insulin can sometimes cause weight gain, avoid overeating and strive to make exercise a part of every day. Above all, work closely with your doctor and diabetes educator to develop a safe and effective weight-loss plan that is tailored to your daily life.

Get moving

Exercise helps you control your blood sugar by making your body more sensitive to insulin, promoting weight loss, and reducing fat around your abdomen. Exercise also lowers blood pressure, reduces your risk of heart disease, improves blood cholesterol levels, and relieves stress.

Try to engage in regular physical activity for 30 to 60 minutes every day. Walking is the form of exercise that doctors recommend most.

Talk with your doctor about the types of physical activity that are best for you. He or she might recommend precautions such as testing your blood glucose before and after exercise and watching for signs of low blood sugar during and after exercise.

Manage your medication

If diet, weight loss, and exercise are not enough to keep your blood sugar level in an acceptable range, your doctor will prescribe a sugar-lowering medication or insulin.

The type of medication you take depends on many factors, including your age, the severity of your diabetes, other health issues, and other medications you are taking. (Some drugs reduce the effectiveness of some diabetes medications.)

Even if you are taking a diabetes medication, a healthy diet and regular exercise are key to managing your condition. Your medication works together with your diet and your exercise program—it doesn't replace them.

CHECK YOUR BLOOD SUGAR

The best way to make sure your blood sugar is in a safe range is to check it frequently.

If you take insulin, your doctor has told you how many times a day you should check your blood sugar. Frequent testing helps you evaluate how well your diet, exercise, and medication are working.

A glycohemoglobin test, performed in the doctor's office or at home, helps your doctor tell how well your diabetes has been controlled over the past few months.

Keep in mind, however, that routine hemoglobin tests are not a substitute for daily blood glucose testing at home.

SETTING NUTRITION GOALS

Although there is no one-size-fits-all diabetic diet, certain healthy eating guidelines apply to everyone who has diabetes. The recipes in this book will help you follow these guidelines.

Because people who have diabetes are at risk of developing heart disease, you need to do more than control your blood sugar levels to stay healthy. Consume a balanced diet that is low in calories, saturated and trans fats, salt, sugar, and alcohol. Choose whole grains over refined ones and add high-fiber vegetables, fruits, and legumes.

The food you eat is composed of carbohydrates, fats, and protein. Carbohydrates and fats are your body's main sources of fuel. Carbs should make up 45 to 65 percent of your daily calories, fats (primarily from vegetable fats) about 20 to 35 percent, and protein about 12 to 20 percent.

HOW TO DISTRIBUTE YOUR DAILY CALORIES

45–65% Carbohydrates 20–35% Fats 12–20% Protein

CARBOHYDRATES

Carbohydrates are the sugars, starches, and fiber that make up foods such as grains, fruits, and vegetables. The total amount of carbohydrate in a meal or snack matters more than whether it's sugar or starch. If you take insulin, adjust the dose before a meal based on how much carbohydrate you plan to eat, because carbohydrates can raise blood sugar quickly.

45–65% OF DAILY CALORIES FROM CARBS

Sugars

Sugars found in many foods include fructose and sucrose (in fruit) and lactose (in milk). Granulated sugar and high-fructose corn syrup are often added to foods and drinks. Sweets do not raise blood sugar faster than do some starches, but they contain few nutrients and little fiber.

Starches

Starches are carbohydrates in bread, grains, cereal, pasta, corn, squash, and potatoes. Whole-grain starches are healthier than refined ones because they provide more vitamins, minerals, and fiber. They also help keep blood sugar steady.

Fiber

Fiber, the indigestible part of plant food, plays a special role in healthy diets. Soluble fiber—found in oats, legumes (beans), barley, and certain fruits and vegetables—not only reduces blood sugar levels but also improves blood cholesterol levels.

ARTIFICIAL SWEETENERS

Carb-free and mostly calorie-free alternatives to sugar can be found in these artificial sweeteners.

ASPARTAME The most widely used sugar substitute, aspartame is 180 times sweeter than sugar. People who cannot tolerate phenyl-alanine should avoid aspartame.

ACESULFAME-K Also known as acesulfame potassium, acesulfame-K is found in baked goods, drinks, frozen desserts, and candy.

SUCRALOSE Sucralose is made from sugar but cannot be digested, so it adds no calories and does not affect blood glucose levels. It is 600 times sweeter than sugar.

NEOTAME Approved for use in a range of products, neotame is 7,000 to 13,000 times sweeter than sugar.

SACCHARIN Although saccharin faced a proposed ban in 1977 because of a possible link to cancer in animals, it remains on the market. Moderate use is considered safe.

HEALTHY FATS

Fats in food help your body store energy and transport some vitamins through the bloodstream. They make food taste smooth and creamy and help make you feel full. Oils from nuts, seeds, and vegetables as well as fats from fish provide health benefits and can reduce your risk of heart disease. These fats, known as unsaturated fats, are usually liquid.

Heart-healthy fats from avocado add rich creaminess to the dressing for Chopped Salad with Lime-Avocado Dressing (page 49).

Monounsaturated fats

Olive, canola, and peanut oils are the main sources of monounsaturated fats, the healthiest fats you can eat. They lower LDL (the so-called bad cholesterol) and raise HDL (good cholesterol) in the blood, helping lower heart disease risk.

Polyunsaturated fats

These fats, which are essential for good health, include corn, sunflower, safflower, flaxseed, and soybeans oils, as well as the oils in fatty fish such as salmon. Rich in omega-3 and omega-6 fatty acids, they lower total cholesterol but also cut HDL (good) cholesterol.

Plant sterols

Nuts, seeds, and many other plant foods contain substances called plant sterols that slow the absorption of dietary cholesterol and can lower LDL (bad) and total cholesterol levels in the blood. Tub margarines and salad dressings with added plant sterols are available in most stores.

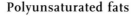

HARMFUL FATS

Not all types of fat are healthy. Saturated and trans fats can increase your risk of heart disease and some forms of cancer. These fats are usually solid or semisolid at room temperature, although they may turn liquid when heated. It's not possible to avoid all harmful fats because they occur in many foods, but it's best to cut back wherever you can.

Saturated fats

Plentiful in meat, dark meat poultry and poultry skin, butter, full-fat dairy products, coconut oil, and palm oil, saturated fats increase total blood cholesterol and LDL (bad) cholesterol. Limit these fats, along with trans fats, to no more than 8 to 10 percent of your total daily calories.

Trans fats

Stick margarine and shortening contain hydrogenated oils that raise total blood cholesterol and LDL (bad) cholesterol levels. These so-called trans fats are common in packaged and processed foods, baked goods, and fried foods such as french fries.

Cholesterol

Egg yolks, liver, shellfish, and full-fat dairy products are rich in cholesterol, which can raise blood cholesterol, although it does not do so in all people. Saturated and trans fats have a greater impact on blood cholesterol than does dietary cholesterol.

FIGURING YOUR FAT

When you are figuring your daily intake of fat (which should be about 30 percent of your total calories each day), consider the total amount of fat eaten during the day, not just in one meal. If you have a big, rich breakfast, for example, limit the amount of fat in your lunch or dinner that day. Here are some other tips.

• Limit fatty meats, full-fat dairy products, and rich baked goods.

• Choose foods made with healthy plant-based fats, such as avocados, olive and canola oils, and nuts.

• Limit your cholesterol intake to less than 300 milligrams a day, or 200 mg if you have heart disease.

• Make some meals meatless.

PROTEIN

12–20% OF DAILY CALORIES FROM PROTEIN

Protein, an essential nutrient found in both plant and animal foods, repairs tissues, builds muscle, and carries hormones and vitamins throughout the body via the bloodstream. Infants and growing children have the highest daily protein requirements, but most Americans consume far more protein than they actually need.

HOW MUCH PROTEIN IS ENOUGH?

Adults need a surprisingly small quantity of protein every day—only 0.8 grams of protein per kilogram (2.2 pounds) of body weight.

There are almost 30 grams of protein in a 3-ounce chicken breast and in a 2-cup bowl of black bean soup. Use your weight to determine how much protein you may need in a day using the chart below.

140 pounds	—	51 grams
150 pounds	—	55 grams
160 pounds	—	59 grams
170 pounds	—	62 grams
180 pounds	—	65 grams

Some people with diabetes have advanced kidney disease and need to limit their daily protein intake to 0.6 grams per kilogram of body weight. To monitor your kidneys' health, your doctor will recommend regular kidney function tests.

Red meats and poultry

Beef, pork, lamb, chicken, and turkey are protein-rich foods that often contain large amounts of harmful saturated fats (page 15), although lean cuts are available. The portions of foods such as beef and chicken in this cookbook are relatively small.

Legumes and fish

Plant proteins such as beans, lentils, peas, and nuts contain healthier fats than do animal proteins, have no cholesterol, and provide healthful fiber. Fish, also a fine protein source, has about as much protein as lean beef, ounce for ounce, but also supplies heart-healthy omega-3 fatty acids.

High-protein diets

Low-carbohydrate, high-protein, high-fat diets can result in rapid weight loss but may cause kidney problems for some people with diabetes. Talk to your doctor and nutritionist if you are thinking about trying a high-protein diet.

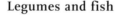

SALT

For some people, consuming too much salt raises blood pressure. High blood pressure is a major risk factor for heart disease and other complications to which people with diabetes are especially vulnerable.

Going low sodium

If you have high blood pressure, your doctor may have asked you to lower your intake of salt. But limiting salt means more than just putting away the salt shaker. It also means staying away from most fast foods and highly salted packaged and canned foods, such as canned soups and vegetables and the flavor packets that come with many packaged dishes.

FLAVOR ENHANCERS

Experiment with herbs and spices, lemon and lime juices, garlic and onion powders, and other sodium-free seasonings. Read food labels carefully to find out exactly how much salt a serving of packaged food provides. Buy reduced-sodium or salt-free canned broths and snack foods such as pretzels.

ALCOHOL

Although moderate drinking can reduce heart attack risk, doctors don't recommend drinking for your health. People with diabetes need to be careful because alcohol interferes with the liver's production of sugar.

Alcohol's impact on blood sugar

If you drink alcohol while taking a diabetes drug that lowers blood sugar or on an empty stomach, your blood sugar could drop dangerously low, and it can remain low for 24 hours, even after just one drink. At other times, the carbs in an alcoholic drink, especially when mixed with something sweet, can raise blood sugar too high.

AFTER DRINKING

Test your blood sugar level after having an alcoholic drink to make sure it is within a safe range—and don't forget to eat. If you have good control of your blood sugar levels, an occasional drink won't hurt. Ask your doctor if it is OK for you to drink and if alcohol interferes with any medications you're taking.

COUNTING CARBOHYDRATES

Because carbohydrates are the main influence on blood sugar, your doctor may suggest keeping track of the grams of carbohydrates you eat each day. This method is newer than using food exchanges, although exchanges are still widely used. How many daily carbohydrate grams are right for you? Follow the three easy steps in the next few pages to estimate your allowance.

HOW TO FIND THE NUTRIENT VALUES IN EACH RECIPE

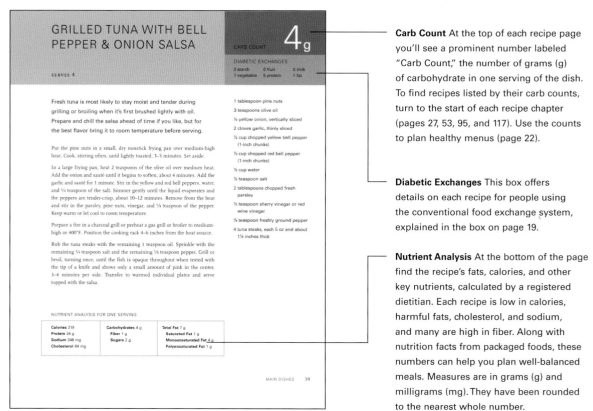

Carb Count At the top of each recipe page you'll see a prominent number labeled "Carb Count," the number of grams (g) of carbohydrate in one serving of the dish. To find recipes listed by their carb counts, turn to the start of each recipe chapter (pages 27, 53, 95, and 117). Use the counts to plan healthy menus (page 22).

Diabetic Exchanges This box offers details on each recipe for people using the conventional food exchange system, explained in the box on page 19.

Nutrient Analysis At the bottom of the page find the recipe's fats, calories, and other key nutrients, calculated by a registered dietitian. Each recipe is low in calories, harmful fats, cholesterol, and sodium, and many are high in fiber. Along with nutrition facts from packaged foods, these numbers can help you plan well-balanced meals. Measures are in grams (g) and milligrams (mg). They have been rounded to the nearest whole number.

1 NOTE YOUR ACTIVITY LEVEL

Your activity level and weight together determine the amount of food you can eat. The more frequent and intense your activities, the more food energy—calories—you burn. Of course, everyday activities such as shopping take less energy than exercise such as jogging. Read the descriptions below to find the one that best describes your activity level.

Take your activity level and go to step 2 →

INACTIVE
Mainly sedentary most days of the week. Daily activities limited to driving, reading, watching television, and cooking, with only rare, light exertion such as shopping.

SOMEWHAT ACTIVE
Low-intensity activity throughout the week. Activities include light housework, leisurely walks, playing with children, climbing stairs at home, low-intensity sports such as golf or bowling.

ACTIVE
Vigorous exercise several days a week. Activities include long brisk walks or bike rides, gardening, mid-intensity sports such as tennis, skiing, softball, swimming, dancing, or yoga.

DIABETIC EXCHANGES

The food exchange system—an alternative way for people with diabetes to plan meals—breaks each serving into nutrients of concern, such as starch, sugar or other carbs, fat, and protein.

Food exchange lists may also show whether the serving contains significant ingredients in the fruit, vegetable, milk, or protein food groups (as shown in this book).

Each exchange is a portion of food that has about the same number of calories as another in its group. In the starch group, for example, a half-cup of corn is the same as half an English muffin. Both would be rated "1 starch" in the Diabetic Exchanges box. That means you can exchange one for the other and keep your calories about the same.

People recently diagnosed with diabetes typically consult with a dietitian and receive daily exchange targets based on their blood sugar levels and daily calorie needs.

Activity's benefits

Regular exercise can help you control your blood sugar level. What's more, less-active people who increase their activity even a little reap many benefits, including improved cholesterol levels, lower blood pressure, sounder sleep, more upbeat mood, increased alertness, and improved memory—and they tend to lose weight. Talk to your doctor or diabetes educator about the right activity for you.

2 FIND YOUR CALORIE NEEDS

The more you weigh, the more calories you need to consume every day. To determine how many calories you can eat each day without gaining or losing pounds, find your weight on the far left side of the chart below; then locate your daily calorie allowance to the right in the column that corresponds to your activity level.

Take your calorie needs and go to step 3 →

LOSE WEIGHT SAFELY

People with diabetes who lose excess weight can improve their blood sugar and have better control of their diabetes. To lose a pound a week—a safe goal—it's necessary to cut about 500 calories a day.

A good approach is to cut back on high-fat, high-sugar, and high-sodium foods and to plan more meals and snacks around whole grains, vegetables, and fruits.

An apple and a chocolate bar both contain about 30 grams of carbohydrate, but the apple is nearly fat-free while the chocolate has 15 grams of fat and 150 more calories.

WEIGHT (in pounds)	INACTIVE	SOMEWHAT ACTIVE	ACTIVE
120	1500	1700	1800
130	1600	1800	1900
140	1700	1900	2100
150	1800	2000	2200
160	2000	2100	2400
170	2100	2300	2500
180	2200	2400	2700
190	2300	2500	2800
200	2500	2700	3000
210	2600	2800	3100
220	2700	3000	3300
230	2800	3100	3400
240	2900	3200	3600
250	3100	3300	3700
260	3200	3500	3900
270	3300	3600	4000
280	3400	3700	4100

CALORIES

3 LOCATE YOUR CARB COUNT

For most people, carbohydrates should make up about 55 percent of their total daily calories. However, your doctor may recommend a lower or higher percentage (see What's Your Carb Percentage? right). In the chart below, locate the box with your daily calorie allowance to find the number of grams (g) of carbohydrates you can eat in a day.

To use your carb count turn the page

CALORIES	CARBS	CALORIES	CARBS	CALORIES	CARBS
1500	210g	2400	330g	3300	455g
1600	220g	2500	345g	3400	470g
1700	235g	2600	360g	3500	480g
1800	250g	2700	370g	3600	495g
1900	260g	2800	385g	3700	510g
2000	275g	2900	400g	3800	525g
2100	290g	3000	415g	3900	540g
2200	300g	3100	425g	4000	550g
2300	315g	3200	440g	4100	565g

WHAT'S YOUR CARB PERCENTAGE?

Because carbohydrates have a greater effect on blood sugar than do other nutrients, your doctor may ask you to adjust the percentage of carbs in your diet. The chart at left shows the number of carb grams that equal 55 percent of total daily calories. If your doctor or diabetes educator has suggested eating less or more, use the following easy formula. Say your daily calorie need is 1800 and your carb percent is 45.

1 Multiply 1800 by 0.45. That equals 810 carb calories per day.

2 Divide your daily carb calories by 4 (the calories in 1 gram of carbohydrate). Your daily carb count is 202 grams.

PLANNING HEALTHY MENUS

Planning menus can be time-consuming when you have diabetes. To help keep your blood sugar steady, it's important to divide up your daily carb count and spread your carb grams throughout the day. You have to measure portions, time your meals, track carbs, and balance it all with exercise and medication. Here's a plan using recipes in this book.

A sample day's menu

Say your carb count is 260 grams and your dietitian has suggested you spread them between three meals and a snack—30 percent for each meal and 10 percent for the snack.

Breakfast (per serving)	78 g
Pineapple Smoothie (page 128)	38 g
Blueberry Bran Muffin (page 132)	26 g
1 cup 1-percent milk	14 g

Lunch (per serving)	78 g
Black Bean Tostada (page 88)	41 g
Chopped Salad with Lime-Avocado Dressing (page 49)	28 g
9 fresh strawberries	9 g

Snack (per serving)	26 g
12 Spicy Pita Chips (page 133)	26 g

Dinner (per serving)	78 g
Spinach & Garlic Lasagne (page 84)	39 g
Roasted Winter Vegetables (page 115)	14 g
Balsamic-Glazed Berries & Tangerines (page 127)	25 g

Day's total	260 g

COOKING FOR GOOD HEALTH

Having healthy ingredients on hand—like low-sodium canned broths and tomatoes in the cupboard, and lean meats and whole-grain bread in the freezer—allows you to put together nutritious meals quickly and easily.

Variety is key

Keep your meals simple but vary your diet by trying new grains, fruits, and vegetables. Experiment with vegetarian dishes. Vegetarians are less likely than meat eaters to develop heart disease, high blood pressure, and obesity, making a meatless diet especially beneficial for people with diabetes. But you need to plan vegetarian meals carefully to ensure that you get sufficient protein and other essential nutrients.

Smart shopping

Take advantage of the many reduced-fat, fat-free, low-sodium, and sugar-free products now in markets. Stock plenty of fresh, frozen, and canned vegetables and fruits (without added sugar). Seek out unsweetened high-fiber cereals and low-fat cheeses. Shop for salt-free "natural" peanut butter and bypass fatty and salty convenience foods. Check labels to find low-fat foods containing 3 grams of fat or fewer for every 100 calories.

Healthier choices in the kitchen

You know it's wise to choose low-fat dairy products over full-fat ones and whole grains over refined ones. Try these other healthy options.

Replace ground meat with beans or soy protein.

Substitute 2 egg whites for each whole egg.

Use soy milk or rice milk instead of cow's milk.

Replace butter, bacon fat, and lard with canola, olive, or peanut oil.

Use lemon juice or vinegar and herbs and spices in place of salt.

Whip evaporated skim milk instead of heavy cream.

Substitute soft tofu for ricotta cheese.

Marinate poultry and meat in nonfat yogurt instead of oil.

WHAT'S A SERVING?

Serving sizes can be confusing. For example, a juice carton may say a serving is 8 ounces, while your recommended serving size is ½ cup, or 4 ounces. Here are some tips for watching how much you eat.

• Use measuring cups and spoons to measure portions or weigh foods on a kitchen scale.

• Weigh bread slices and bagel halves to make sure they fit into your carb count. If they're too large, cut them into smaller pieces.

• Divide and weigh meat and poultry portions before cooking. A 3-ounce piece is about the size of your palm.

FOODS THAT FIGHT DIABETES

INGREDIENT	CONTAINS	HEALTH BENEFIT
Oats • legumes • vegetables • dried fruit • whole grains • berries and other fresh fruit	Fiber	Helps control weight; promotes healthy digestion; soluble fiber improves cholesterol and lowers blood sugar.
Fruits and vegetables • nuts • vegetable oils • wheat germ • fish and seafood	Antioxidants	Fight cell damaging free radicals, which are produced when blood sugar is high and may contribute to complications of diabetes.
Nuts and seeds • corn oil and soybean oil • tub margarines with added sterols	Plant sterols	Lower cholesterol levels.
Legumes • fish • poultry • lean meats • low-fat dairy products • low-fat tofu	Low-fat protein	Builds, maintains, and repairs body tissues.
Salmon • sardines • mackerel • herring • flaxseed and flaxseed oil	Omega-3 fatty acids	Reduce heart disease risk by improving cholesterol and preventing blood clots; reduce joint pain and inflammation.
Dark green leafy vegetables • fruits • legumes • wheat germ • whole grains	Folic acid	Reduces heart risk by reducing homocysteine in the blood; helps form blood cells; essential in pregnancy for preventing birth defects.

INGREDIENT	CONTAINS	HEALTH BENEFIT
Onions and garlic • chives • shallots • leeks	Allicin	A sulfur-containing substance that may lower cholesterol, reduce blood-clotting, and control blood pressure.
Dairy products • fortified juices • fortified breakfast cereals • legumes • canned fish (with bones)	Calcium	Essential for transmitting nerve impulses, regulating heart rhythm, and enhancing muscle function; maintains bone strength.
Bran cereals • whole grains • green beans • broccoli • spices • processed meats	Chromium	Enhances insulin's effects in converting sugar, protein, and fat into energy; works with insulin to transport sugar from the blood into cells.
Spinach and beet greens • nuts • whole grains • legumes • dairy products • fish • meat • poultry	Magnesium	Helps lower blood pressure; helps prevent irregular heartbeat; more is needed when blood sugar is high and when taking diuretics.
Whole grains • sunflower seeds • oysters • gelatin • vegetable oil • corn • parsley • green beans • soy	Vanadium	A trace mineral that promotes insulin production and increases the body's sensitivity to insulin.
Shellfish • red meat • legumes • nuts • eggs • tofu and other soy foods • wheat germ	Zinc	Needed for the breakdown of protein, fat, and carbohydrates; helps make protein and insulin; essential for growth and development.

STARTERS, SOUPS & SALADS

Carb Count	Item
2g	SMOKED SALMON WITH CUCUMBER & DILL, 31
6g	HOT & SOUR SOUP, 36
9g	ASPARAGUS WITH SHALLOTS & BLUE CHEESE, 46
14g	BEET & SPINACH SALAD, 50
15g	CHICKEN SOUP WITH ROSEMARY & GARLIC, 42
16g	MUSHROOM BARLEY SOUP, 37
17g	VEGETABLE SOUP WITH BASIL & PINE NUTS, 39
17g	BIBB LETTUCE SALAD WITH ORANGE & AVOCADO, 45

Carb Count	Item
21g	VEGETABLE PLATTER WITH HUMMUS DIP, 34
23g	RED LENTIL SOUP, 41
24g	TOMATOES STUFFED WITH CUCUMBER & FETA CHEESE, 33
27g	RED BELL PEPPER QUESADILLAS, 28
28g	CHOPPED SALAD WITH LIME-AVOCADO DRESSING, 49
30g	BULGUR SALAD WITH ARUGULA & OLIVES, 48

Bibb Lettuce Salad with Orange & Avocado, 45

RED BELL PEPPER QUESADILLAS

DIABETIC EXCHANGES

| 1½ starch | 0 fruit | 0 milk |
| ½ vegetable | ½ protein | ½ fat |

SERVES 4

1½ teaspoons olive oil or canola oil

½ cup diced red bell pepper

2 green onions, thinly sliced, about ½ cup

2 tablespoons minced fresh cilantro

2 teaspoons seeded diced jalapeño chile, or to taste

8 corn tortillas, 6 inches in diameter

6 tablespoons shredded Monterey Jack cheese

These toasty quesadillas can be mild or spicy—simply vary the amount of jalapeño. For an extra-light version, replace the Jack cheese with *queso asadero*, a mild, low-fat Mexican cheese. Look for it in well-stocked supermarkets and Latin groceries.

In a large frying pan, warm ½ teaspoon of the oil over medium heat until hot. Stir in the bell pepper and sauté until the pepper begins to soften, 2–3 minutes. Stir in the green onions and sauté for 1 minute. Remove from the heat and stir in the cilantro and jalapeño. Transfer the mixture to a small bowl. Reserve the frying pan to use again.

Place 4 of the corn tortillas on a countertop or cutting board. Sprinkle each tortilla with 1 tablespoon of the cheese, then top each one with one-fourth of the bell pepper mixture, another ½ tablespoon of the cheese, and the 4 remaining tortillas.

With a pastry brush, brush the remaining 1 teaspoon oil over the tops of the tortillas. Place the frying pan over medium heat. Carefully add 2 filled tortillas and cook until lightly browned, 2–3 minutes per side. Repeat with the 2 remaining filled tortillas. Cut the quesadillas into quarters, divide the quarters among individual plates, and serve immediately.

NUTRIENT ANALYSIS FOR ONE SERVING

Calories 180	Carbohydrates 27 g	Total Fat 6 g
Protein 6 g	Fiber 3 g	Saturated Fat 2 g
Sodium 144 mg	Sugars 1 g	Monounsaturated Fat 1 g
Cholesterol 9 mg		Polyunsaturated Fat 1 g

SMOKED SALMON WITH CUCUMBER & DILL

SERVES 4

This elegant starter can be prepared in less than 10 minutes. It features thin slices of heart-healthy salmon flavored lightly with spicy mustard. Compare brands of packaged cured salmon to find the one with the lowest sodium content.

Spread the mustard lightly on one side of each salmon slice. On each individual salad plate, place 1 lettuce leaf. Set aside.

Cut the cucumber diagonally into thin slices and arrange them in a single layer over the lettuce.

For each serving, arrange 2 salmon slices on top of the cucumber slices and garnish with chopped dill.

2 teaspoons coarse-grained or Dijon mustard

¼ lb thinly sliced smoked salmon, cut into 8 pieces

4 leaves butter (Boston) or red-leaf lettuce

½ large English cucumber, 5–6 oz

2 tablespoons chopped fresh dill

NUTRIENT ANALYSIS FOR ONE SERVING

Calories 35	**Carbohydrates** 2 g	**Total Fat** 1 g
Protein 6 g	**Fiber** 1 g	**Saturated Fat** 0 g
Sodium 390 mg	**Sugars** 1 g	**Monounsaturated Fat** 0 g
Cholesterol 10 mg		**Polyunsaturated Fat** 0 g

TOMATOES STUFFED WITH CUCUMBER & FETA CHEESE

SERVES 4

CARB COUNT 24g

DIABETIC EXCHANGES

| 1 starch | 0 fruit | 0 milk |
| 2 vegetable | ½ protein | 1 fat |

Fresh herbs and vegetables tossed with bulgur, a chewy whole grain that's quick and easy to prepare, make a healthful filling for these Mediterranean-style stuffed tomatoes. Substitute cooked brown rice for the prepared bulgur if you like.

In a bowl, combine the bulgur, boiling water, and lemon juice. Let stand until most of the liquid has been absorbed, about 30 minutes. Add the cucumber, red onion, 3 tablespoons of the feta cheese, green and red bell peppers, parsley, and oregano; toss gently to mix.

In a separate small bowl, combine the red wine vinegar, olive oil, pepper, and salt. Whisk until well blended. Drizzle the vinaigrette over the bulgur mixture and toss gently to blend. Cover and refrigerate until ready to use.

Just before serving, cut off the tops of the tomatoes. Reserve the tops. With a spoon or melon baller, scoop out and discard the tomato seeds and ribs.

Remove the bulgur mixture from the refrigerator and, with a spoon, divide the mixture evenly among the scooped-out tomatoes. Sprinkle the remaining 1 tablespoon feta cheese over the top of the filling and garnish with the tomato tops.

½ cup bulgur

⅓ cup boiling water

2 tablespoons fresh lemon juice

¼ small cucumber, peeled, seeded, and diced (about ⅓ cup)

3 tablespoons diced red onion

4 tablespoons crumbled feta cheese

2 tablespoons diced green bell pepper

2 tablespoons diced red bell pepper

2 tablespoons chopped fresh parsley

½ tablespoon chopped fresh oregano or 1 teaspoon dried oregano

1 tablespoon red wine vinegar

2½ teaspoons olive oil

¼ teaspoon freshly ground pepper

⅛ teaspoon salt

4 large red, yellow, or orange tomatoes, about 1½ lb total weight

NUTRIENT ANALYSIS FOR ONE SERVING

Calories 156	Carbohydrates 24 g	Total Fat 6 g
Protein 8 g	Fiber 6 g	Saturated Fat 2 g
Sodium 198 mg	Sugars 6 g	Monounsaturated Fat 3 g
Cholesterol 8 mg		Polyunsaturated Fat 1 g

VEGETABLE PLATTER WITH HUMMUS DIP

SERVES 6

1½ cups broccoli florets

1½ cups cauliflower florets

2 large cloves garlic

One 15-oz can chickpeas (garbanzo beans), rinsed and drained

⅓ lb reduced-fat silken tofu, cut into ½-inch cubes

3 tablespoons fresh lemon juice

1 tablespoon chopped fresh mint or 1 teaspoon dried mint, plus several fresh mint sprigs (optional)

2 teaspoons olive oil

1 teaspoon dark sesame oil

½ teaspoon red pepper flakes

¼ teaspoon salt

2 red or yellow bell peppers, or 1 of each, cut into large chunks

1½ cups baby carrots

The vegetables in this appetizer taste delicious with hummus, a Middle Eastern dip made of chickpeas, sesame, lemon, and garlic. You can substitute ⅔ cup dried chickpeas for the canned beans. (For tips on cooking dried beans, see page 135.)

Bring a large saucepan three-fourths full of water to a boil. Add the broccoli and cauliflower and return to a boil. Cook until the vegetables are tender-crisp, about 1 minute. Drain the vegetables and then plunge them into a bowl of ice water to stop the cooking. Drain again and set aside.

In a food processor or blender, process the garlic until minced. Add the chickpeas and process until finely chopped. Add the tofu, lemon juice, chopped mint, 1 teaspoon of the olive oil, sesame oil, red pepper flakes, and salt and process until smooth. Transfer the hummus to a serving bowl and drizzle with the remaining 1 teaspoon olive oil.

To serve, arrange the broccoli, cauliflower, bell peppers, and carrots on a serving platter and garnish with the mint sprigs, if desired. Place the bowl of hummus alongside as a dip for the vegetables.

NUTRIENT ANALYSIS FOR ONE SERVING

Calories 138	**Carbohydrates** 21 g	**Total Fat** 4 g
Protein 7 g	**Fiber** 6 g	**Saturated Fat** 1 g
Sodium 140 mg	**Sugars** 4 g	**Monounsaturated Fat** 2 g
Cholesterol 0 mg		**Polyunsaturated Fat** 1 g

6g

HOT & SOUR SOUP

SERVES 6

- ⅓ lb reduced-fat, extra-firm tofu, cut into ½-inch cubes
- 3 tablespoons low-sodium soy sauce
- 2 teaspoons dark sesame oil
- 6 oz fresh shiitake mushrooms, brushed clean, stemmed, and sliced
- 4½ cups fat-free, no-salt-added chicken broth
- 1 cup snow peas, thawed if frozen, trimmed and cut lengthwise into thin strips
- 3 tablespoons rice vinegar
- ½ teaspoon red pepper flakes or 1 teaspoon hot chile oil
- 2 tablespoons cornstarch
- 2 tablespoons water
- ¼ cup chopped fresh cilantro or thinly sliced green onion

This crowd-pleasing soup is remarkably easy to prepare and goes from stove to table in less than 15 minutes. Fresh shiitake mushrooms give the soup a delicate flavor, but you can use readily available button mushrooms as a delicious alternative.

Toss the tofu with the soy sauce and set aside.

In a large saucepan, heat the sesame oil over medium heat until hot. Add the mushrooms and cook, stirring occasionally, until the mushrooms are tender, about 5 minutes. Add the broth, snow peas, vinegar, and red pepper flakes to the saucepan with the mushrooms. Bring to a boil over high heat. Reduce the heat to low and simmer, uncovered, for 5 minutes.

Combine the cornstarch and water and stir to mix well. Add the cornstarch mixture to the soup and simmer until the soup is thickened, about 1 minute. Add the tofu mixture, return to a simmer, and cook until heated through, about 1 minute. Stir in the cilantro and serve.

NUTRIENT ANALYSIS FOR ONE SERVING

Calories 82	**Carbohydrates** 6 g	**Total Fat** 2 g
Protein 8 g	**Fiber** 1 g	**Saturated Fat** 0 g
Sodium 461 mg	**Sugars** 1 g	**Monounsaturated Fat** 1 g
Cholesterol 0 mg		**Polyunsaturated Fat** 1 g

MUSHROOM BARLEY SOUP

CARB COUNT 16g

DIABETIC EXCHANGES
½ starch   0 fruit   0 milk
1½ vegetable   1 protein   ½ fat

SERVES 6

Fresh and dried mushrooms contribute subtle woodsy flavors and aromas to this satisfying soup. Find dried mushrooms in the produce section of your supermarket. Use kitchen shears to snip them into small pieces before soaking.

In a small heatproof glass measuring cup or bowl, combine the dried porcini and boiling water. Let stand for 20 minutes. Remove the porcini with a slotted spoon and set aside. Line a fine-mesh sieve with a paper coffee filter or cheesecloth and strain the porcini soaking liquid to remove the grit; reserve the liquid.

While the porcini are soaking, in a large saucepan, heat the olive oil over medium-high heat. Add the shallots and cook, stirring occasionally, until softened, about 3 minutes. Add the sliced fresh mushrooms and cook, stirring occasionally, until lightly browned, about 3 minutes. Add the broth, barley, and carrots and bring to a simmer. Reduce the heat to low. Add the porcini, reserved porcini soaking liquid, thyme, bay leaf, salt, and pepper. Simmer, uncovered, stirring occasionally, until the barley is tender, about 25 minutes. Remove the bay leaf and serve.

3 tablespoons snipped or chopped dried porcini mushrooms

1 cup boiling water

2 teaspoons olive oil

½ cup chopped shallots

½ lb fresh cremini or button mushrooms, sliced, or packaged sliced mixed fresh mushrooms such as oyster, cremini, and shiitake

6 cups fat-free, no-salt-added beef broth

½ cup quick-cooking pearl barley

½ cup thinly sliced carrots

1 tablespoon chopped fresh thyme or 1 teaspoon dried thyme

1 bay leaf

¾ teaspoon salt

¼ teaspoon freshly ground pepper

NUTRIENT ANALYSIS FOR ONE SERVING

Calories 111	**Carbohydrates** 16 g	**Total Fat** 2 g
Protein 9 g	**Fiber** 3 g	**Saturated Fat** 0 g
Sodium 478 mg	**Sugars** 2 g	**Monounsaturated Fat** 1 g
Cholesterol 0 mg		**Polyunsaturated Fat** 0 g

VEGETABLE SOUP WITH BASIL & PINE NUTS

CARB COUNT 17g

DIABETIC EXCHANGES
| ½ starch | 0 fruit | 0 milk |
| 2 vegetable | ½ protein | ½ fat |

SERVES 6

This simple dish is based on a classic vegetable stew known as *soupe au pistou* in France. It gets a burst of flavor from fresh basil. If fresh fennel isn't available, use two chopped celery stalks or ½ pound of green beans, trimmed and cut into pieces.

Put the pine nuts in a small, dry nonstick frying pan over medium-high heat. Cook, stirring often, until lightly toasted, 3–5 minutes. Set aside.

In a large saucepan, heat the olive oil over medium-high heat. Add the onion, fennel, and garlic and sauté until fragrant, about 5 minutes. Stir in the potatoes and broth. Cover and bring to a simmer over high heat. Reduce the heat to low and simmer, covered, until the vegetables are just tender, 18–20 minutes. Stir in the chopped tomato, salt, and pepper and continue to simmer until the tomato is softened, about 2 minutes.

While the soup is simmering, in a food processor or blender, combine the basil leaves and toasted pine nuts. Process until very finely chopped. Stir the mixture into the soup and ladle the soup into individual bowls.

3 tablespoons pine nuts

1 teaspoon olive oil

1 yellow onion, chopped

1 fennel bulb, chopped

3 cloves garlic, minced

½ lb red potatoes, cut into ½-inch pieces

4 cups fat-free, no-salt-added vegetable or chicken broth

1 large tomato, seeded and chopped

¼ teaspoon salt

¼ teaspoon freshly ground pepper

⅓ cup packed fresh basil leaves

NUTRIENT ANALYSIS FOR ONE SERVING

Calories 109	Carbohydrates 17 g	Total Fat 3 g
Protein 4 g	Fiber 4 g	Saturated Fat 0 g
Sodium 430 mg	Sugars 5 g	Monounsaturated Fat 1 g
Cholesterol 0 mg		Polyunsaturated Fat 1 g

RED LENTIL SOUP

SERVES 6

Quick-cooking red lentils have a mild flavor that pairs nicely with curry powder. If you can't find Madras curry, use regular curry powder and add a pinch of cayenne. Brown lentils may be substituted; simmer the soup 8 to 10 minutes longer.

In a large saucepan, heat the oil over medium heat. Add the onion and garlic and cook, stirring occasionally, until soft and fragrant, about 5 minutes. Sprinkle the curry powder and cardamom over the onion mixture and cook, stirring, for 1 minute longer.

Add the broth, lentils, and salt and bring to a boil over high heat. Reduce the heat to low and simmer, uncovered, stirring occasionally, until the lentils are tender, 20–25 minutes. Stir in the Swiss chard and cook, stirring once, until the chard is tender, about 5 minutes. Ladle into individual shallow bowls and top with the yogurt and cilantro.

2 teaspoons olive oil or canola oil

1 yellow onion, chopped

4 cloves garlic, minced

2 teaspoons Madras or hot curry powder

½ teaspoon ground cardamom

5 cups fat-free, no-salt-added chicken or vegetable broth

¾ cup dried red lentils

¾ teaspoon salt

3 cups coarsely chopped Swiss chard or kale

¼ cup low-fat plain yogurt

¼ cup chopped fresh cilantro

NUTRIENT ANALYSIS FOR ONE SERVING

Calories 164	**Carbohydrates** 23 g	**Total Fat** 2 g
Protein 10 g	**Fiber** 6 g	**Saturated Fat** 0 g
Sodium 490 mg	**Sugars** 4 g	**Monounsaturated Fat** 1 g
Cholesterol 1 mg		**Polyunsaturated Fat** 0 g

CHICKEN SOUP WITH ROSEMARY & GARLIC

DIABETIC EXCHANGES

1 starch	0 fruit	0 milk
0 vegetable	2½ protein	½ fat

SERVES 6

2 teaspoons olive oil

4 cloves garlic, minced

½ lb skinless, boneless chicken breast halves, cut into ½-inch chunks

2 zucchini or yellow crookneck squash, or 1 of each, cut into ½-inch chunks

1 tablespoon chopped fresh rosemary or 1 teaspoon dried rosemary

½ teaspoon salt

¼ teaspoon freshly ground pepper

4 cups fat-free, no-salt-added chicken broth

6 slices whole-wheat baguette, ½ inch thick, toasted

6 tablespoons grated Asiago or Romano cheese

Rich with the irresistible flavors of Tuscany—olive oil, garlic, rosemary, and a bit of freshly grated cheese—this soup is hearty enough to serve as a main course or as a substantial first course in a dinner with a light pasta dish and a salad.

In a saucepan, heat the olive oil over medium heat. Add the garlic and sauté for 2 minutes. Add the chicken, squash, rosemary, salt, and pepper and sauté for 2 minutes. Add the broth and bring to a simmer over high heat. Reduce the heat to low and simmer, uncovered, until the chicken is cooked through and the squash is tender, about 8 minutes.

Ladle the soup into individual bowls and top each serving with a slice of toasted baguette and 1 tablespoon of the cheese.

NUTRIENT ANALYSIS FOR ONE SERVING

Calories 177	**Carbohydrates** 15 g	**Total Fat** 5 g
Protein 18 g	**Fiber** 3 g	**Saturated Fat** 2 g
Sodium 491 mg	**Sugars** 2 g	**Monounsaturated Fat** 2 g
Cholesterol 28 mg		**Polyunsaturated Fat** 1 g

BIBB LETTUCE SALAD WITH ORANGE & AVOCADO

SERVES 4

In this classic tossed salad, chunks of creamy, mild avocado contrast deliciously with the intense sweet-and-sour tang of fresh orange. You can use 1 large orange instead of small navel oranges, and cut the peeled segments in half.

In a large bowl, combine the lettuce, avocado, and orange segments.

In a small bowl, combine the orange juice, shallots, mustard, salt, and pepper and stir to mix well.

Pour the orange juice mixture over the lettuce mixture and toss well. Transfer to individual plates and serve immediately.

1 small head Bibb or butter (Boston) lettuce, torn into pieces

½ ripe avocado, pitted, peeled, and cut into ¾-inch chunks

2 small navel oranges, peeled and separated into segments

¼ cup orange juice

1 tablespoon minced shallots

2 teaspoons honey mustard

¼ teaspoon salt

¼ teaspoon freshly ground pepper

NUTRIENT ANALYSIS FOR ONE SERVING

Calories 103	**Carbohydrates** 17 g	**Total Fat** 4 g
Protein 3 g	**Fiber** 5 g	**Saturated Fat** 1 g
Sodium 159 mg	**Sugars** 11 g	**Monounsaturated Fat** 2 g
Cholesterol 0 mg		**Polyunsaturated Fat** 1 g

9g

ASPARAGUS WITH SHALLOTS & BLUE CHEESE

SERVES 4

½ whole-wheat English muffin, torn into chunks

1 teaspoon walnut oil or olive oil

2 tablespoons minced shallot or sweet onion

16 asparagus spears, trimmed

3 tablespoons fat-free, no-salt-added chicken broth

1 tablespoon white wine vinegar or sherry vinegar

⅛ teaspoon salt

¼ teaspoon freshly ground pepper

4 large leaves red-leaf lettuce

1½ tablespoons crumbled Gorgonzola or other blue cheese

Served at room temperature, this salad of asparagus and fresh greens goes well with a dish such as Seared Sirloin with Sweet Potato Ragout (page 73). The salad and dressing can be made up to 2 hours ahead; refrigerate them separately until serving.

Place the English muffin chunks in a food processor or blender and process to coarse crumbs. Heat the oil in a large nonstick frying pan over high heat. Add the minced shallot and sauté, stirring occasionally, until tender, about 3 minutes. Add the muffin crumbs and continue cooking, stirring constantly, until the shallots and crumbs are crisp, 2–3 minutes. Remove from the heat and let stand while preparing the salad.

In a large pot fitted with a steamer basket, bring 1 inch of water to a boil. Add the asparagus, cover, and steam until the asparagus is tender-crisp, about 4 minutes. Drain the asparagus, then plunge the spears into a bowl of ice water to stop the cooking. Drain again and set aside.

In a small bowl, combine the broth, vinegar, salt, and pepper and mix well.

Place 1 lettuce leaf on each plate. Arrange 4 asparagus spears on each lettuce leaf and top with the crumb mixture and cheese. Stir the dressing and drizzle it evenly over the salads.

NUTRIENT ANALYSIS FOR ONE SERVING

Calories 64	Carbohydrates 9 g	Total Fat 2 g
Protein 4 g	Fiber 2 g	Saturated Fat 1 g
Sodium 186 mg	Sugars 2 g	Monounsaturated Fat 0 g
Cholesterol 2 mg		Polyunsaturated Fat 1 g

BULGUR SALAD WITH ARUGULA & OLIVES

SERVES 4

1 cup bulgur

1½ cups boiling water

⅓ cup fat-free, no-salt-added chicken or vegetable broth

2 tablespoons fresh lemon juice

1 tablespoon olive oil

¼ teaspoon freshly ground pepper

1 large tomato or 2 plum (Roma) tomatoes, seeded and chopped

1 cup packed coarsely chopped arugula or watercress

¼ cup sliced pitted Kalamata olives

2 tablespoons chopped fresh mint

Traditionally made with parsley, the Mediterranean salad called tabbouleh takes on a hint of Italy when made instead with arugula, a mustard-family green. Chop the vegetables while the bulgur soaks and serve the salad at room temperature.

Place the bulgur in a large, heatproof bowl and add the boiling water. Let stand until the bulgur is tender and the water is completely absorbed, about 25 minutes.

Add the broth, lemon juice, olive oil, pepper, tomato, arugula, olives, and mint. Toss gently just until the ingredients are evenly distributed. Serve at room temperature, or cover and refrigerate for up to 2 hours.

NUTRIENT ANALYSIS FOR ONE SERVING

Calories 188	**Carbohydrates** 30 g	**Total Fat** 6 g
Protein 5 g	**Fiber** 7 g	**Saturated Fat** 1 g
Sodium 181 mg	**Sugars** 2 g	**Monounsaturated Fat** 4 g
Cholesterol 0 mg		**Polyunsaturated Fat** 1 g

CHOPPED SALAD WITH LIME-AVOCADO DRESSING

CARB COUNT 28g

DIABETIC EXCHANGES
½ starch   0 fruit   0 milk
1½ vegetable 0 protein   1 fat

SERVES 4

Compatible ingredients including tomatoes, fresh corn, cumin, jalapeños, and freshly toasted tortilla chips give this salad an appealing south-of-the-border flavor. A bit of chicken broth lightens the dressing. Serve alongside roasted or grilled fish.

Preheat the oven to 400°F. Stack the tortillas and cut them into quarters to form 16 wedges. Arrange the wedges in a single layer on a baking sheet. Bake until golden brown and crisp, 10–12 minutes. Transfer the toasted tortilla wedges to a plate; set aside.

While the tortillas are toasting, line each individual plate with 2 lettuce leaves, cut or torn in half, if necessary, to fit. In a large bowl, combine the chopped lettuce, tomato, carrot, and corn. In a food processor or blender, combine the avocado, jalapeño, broth, lime juice, canola oil, cumin, and salt and process until puréed. Add the dressing to the chopped lettuce mixture and toss to coat. Divide the salad among the lettuce-lined plates. Garnish with the tortilla chips.

4 corn tortillas, 6 inches in diameter

1 head romaine lettuce, 8 outer leaves left whole, remaining inner leaves coarsely chopped (about 2 cups)

1 large tomato, chopped

1 large carrot, cut into julienne or coarsely grated

1 cup fresh or frozen corn kernels, thawed

½ cup diced pitted peeled avocado

1 jalapeño chile, seeded and chopped

2 tablespoons fat-free, no-salt-added chicken or vegetable broth

1 tablespoon fresh lime juice

1 teaspoon canola oil

½ teaspoon ground cumin

¼ teaspoon salt

NUTRIENT ANALYSIS FOR ONE SERVING

Calories 161	**Carbohydrates** 28 g	**Total Fat** 5 g
Protein 5 g	**Fiber** 6 g	**Saturated Fat** 1 g
Sodium 167 mg	**Sugars** 3 g	**Monounsaturated Fat** 3 g
Cholesterol 0 mg		**Polyunsaturated Fat** 1 g

BEET & SPINACH SALAD

SERVES 4

4 beets, about 1¼ lb total weight

½ cup water

6 cups packed baby spinach
  or torn spinach leaves

3 tablespoons fat-free, no-salt-
  added chicken or vegetable broth

2½ tablespoons balsamic vinegar

1 teaspoon olive oil

1 tablespoon honey mustard

¼ teaspoon freshly ground pepper

⅛ teaspoon salt

2 tablespoons dry-roasted,
  unsalted pistachios or toasted
  pine nuts (page 138)

Plenty colorful to begin with, this light salad looks even bolder and brighter when made with a mixture of red and golden beets, or with Chioggia beets, which have brilliant, striped flesh. Look for uncommon beet varieties at farmers' markets.

Preheat the oven to 375°F. Trim off the beet greens and reserve for another use. Rinse the beets well and arrange them, unpeeled, in a single layer in a shallow baking dish. Add the water and cover the dish with aluminum foil. Roast until the beets are tender, 35–45 minutes.

Transfer the roasted beets to a colander and rinse with cold water. Let stand until cool enough to handle. With a small sharp knife, peel the beets and cut them into slices about ⅛ inch thick.

Combine the beet slices and spinach in a large bowl. In a separate bowl, combine the broth, vinegar, olive oil, mustard, pepper, and salt and stir to mix well. Add the broth-vinegar mixture to the spinach-beet mixture and toss well to coat. Transfer to individual plates and top with the pistachios.

NUTRIENT ANALYSIS FOR ONE SERVING

Calories 101	**Carbohydrates** 14 g	**Total Fat** 4 g
Protein 4 g	**Fiber** 3 g	**Saturated Fat** 1 g
Sodium 191 mg	**Sugars** 10 g	**Monounsaturated Fat** 2 g
Cholesterol 0 mg		**Polyunsaturated Fat** 1 g

MAIN DISHES

Chicken with Caramelized Onions, 64

OVEN-BARBECUED SALMON

SERVES 4

¼ cup orange juice

2 tablespoons fresh lemon juice

4 skinless salmon fillets, each 5 oz and about 1¼ inches thick

1 tablespoon firmly packed light brown sugar

1 tablespoon paprika

½ teaspoon salt

½ teaspoon garlic powder

½ teaspoon onion powder

½ teaspoon ground coriander

¼ teaspoon ground cinnamon

¼ teaspoon cayenne pepper

⅛ teaspoon ground cumin

½ teaspoon canola oil

Tangy citrus juices blended with a range of spices make a complex, barbecue-style rub that complements the rich flavor of baked salmon. Although the list of spices is long, it takes just a minute or two to combine the ingredients for this satisfying dish.

In a large shallow nonaluminum container or lock-top plastic bag, combine the orange and lemon juices. Add the salmon fillets, turn to coat, cover or seal the container, and refrigerate for 30 minutes.

In a small bowl, combine the brown sugar, paprika, salt, garlic powder, onion powder, coriander, cinnamon, cayenne, and cumin.

Preheat the oven to 400°F.

Lightly coat the bottom of a shallow baking dish with the canola oil. Remove the fish from the marinade and pat dry with paper towels. Discard the marinade. Place the fish in the oiled baking dish. Rub the top and sides of the fish with the spice mixture. Bake until the fish is opaque throughout when tested in the center with the tip of a knife, 10–12 minutes. Transfer the baked fillets to warmed individual plates and serve immediately.

NUTRIENT ANALYSIS FOR ONE SERVING

Calories 228	**Carbohydrates** 5 g	**Total Fat** 10 g
Protein 29 g	**Fiber** 1 g	**Saturated Fat** 1 g
Sodium 358 mg	**Sugars** 3 g	**Monounsaturated Fat** 3 g
Cholesterol 78 mg		**Polyunsaturated Fat** 4 g

DIABETIC EXCHANGES

0 starch	0 fruit	0 milk
½ vegetable	4 protein	1 fat

SERVES 4

10 large basil leaves

¼ cup coarsely chopped spinach

2 tablespoons coarsely chopped parsley

1 tablespoon coarsely chopped almonds

1 clove garlic, minced

2 teaspoons olive oil or canola oil

2 teaspoons lemon juice

¼ teaspoon salt

¼ teaspoon freshly ground pepper

4 grouper fillets, each 5 oz and about 1¼ inches thick

20 large spinach leaves, each about 5 by 6 inches, tough stems removed

1 lemon, sliced into 12 thin circles

Any firm, white-fleshed fish works well in this elegant dish. Fillets are topped with a simple basil-almond pesto, wrapped in spinach leaves, and baked. A store-bought pesto can stand in for homemade, but it will likely be higher in fat and calories.

Preheat the oven to 375°F.

In a small food processor or blender, combine the basil, chopped spinach, parsley, almonds, garlic, oil, lemon juice, and ⅛ teaspoon of the salt. Pulse to blend.

Sprinkle the remaining ⅛ teaspoon salt and the pepper on the grouper. Top each fillet with a dollop of pesto.

Place 5 spinach leaves on a paper towel and microwave 15 seconds on high or until the spinach wilts but is still bright green; let cool slightly. On a cutting board or flat surface, arrange 3 wilted spinach leaves, overlapping them slightly. Place a pesto-topped fish fillet in the center of the leaves. Top with 2 more spinach leaves, making sure to cover the fish completely. Using your fingers, press the leaves together to seal. Repeat the procedure with the remaining spinach leaves and fish. Place 3 lemon slices across the top of each spinach-wrapped fillet, overlapping them slightly.

Place the wrapped fillets on a baking sheet lined with parchment paper or aluminum foil. Bake until the fish is firm to the touch, about 15 minutes. Serve immediately.

NUTRIENT ANALYSIS FOR ONE SERVING

Calories 186	Carbohydrates 3 g	Total Fat 6 g
Protein 30 g	Fiber 2 g	Saturated Fat 1 g
Sodium 265 mg	Sugars 0 g	Monounsaturated Fat 3 g
Cholesterol 52 mg		Polyunsaturated Fat 1 g

CORNMEAL-CRUSTED SNAPPER FILLETS

CARB COUNT

8g

DIABETIC EXCHANGES

| ½ starch | 0 fruit | 0 milk |
| 0 vegetable | 4½ protein | 1 fat |

SERVES 4

Dusted with spiced cornmeal and browned, the snapper in this recipe cooks up crisp outside and tender inside. Other thin fillets of fish, such as cod, orange roughy, or pollack, also work well in this dish. Try it paired with Soybean Succotash (page 102).

In a shallow dish, combine the cornmeal, parsley, paprika, salt, garlic powder, onion flakes, and cayenne. Stir to blend.

In another shallow dish, combine the egg whites and water, and whisk to blend. Dip the fish in the egg whites, then dredge in the cornmeal mixture to coat.

In a large nonstick frying pan, heat the oil over medium-high heat. Add the fish and cook, turning once, until the fish is opaque throughout when tested in the center with a tip of a knife and the coating is lightly browned, 2–3 minutes per side.

¼ cup yellow cornmeal

2 tablespoons minced fresh parsley

1 teaspoon paprika

¼ teaspoon salt

½ teaspoon garlic powder

½ teaspoon minced onion flakes

⅛ teaspoon cayenne pepper

2 egg whites, lightly beaten

1 tablespoon water

4 skinless snapper fillets, each 5 oz and about ½ inch thick

1½ tablespoons olive oil or canola oil

NUTRIENT ANALYSIS FOR ONE SERVING

Calories 231	**Carbohydrates** 8 g	**Total Fat** 7 g
Protein 32 g	**Fiber** 1 g	**Saturated Fat** 1 g
Sodium 265 mg	**Sugars** 0 g	**Monounsaturated Fat** 3 g
Cholesterol 52 mg		**Polyunsaturated Fat** 2 g

GRILLED TUNA WITH BELL PEPPER & ONION SALSA

CARB COUNT 4 g

DIABETIC EXCHANGES
| 0 starch | 0 fruit | 0 milk |
| 1 vegetable | 5 protein | 1 fat |

SERVES 4

Fresh tuna is most likely to stay moist and tender during grilling or broiling when it's first brushed lightly with oil. Prepare and chill the salsa ahead of time if you like, but for the best flavor bring it to room temperature before serving.

Put the pine nuts in a small, dry nonstick frying pan over medium-high heat. Cook, stirring often, until lightly toasted, 3–5 minutes. Set aside.

In a large frying pan, heat 2 teaspoons of the olive oil over medium heat. Add the onion and sauté until it begins to soften, about 4 minutes. Add the garlic and sauté for 1 minute. Stir in the yellow and red bell peppers, water, and ¼ teaspoon of the salt. Simmer gently until the liquid evaporates and the peppers are tender-crisp, about 10–12 minutes. Remove from the heat and stir in the parsley, pine nuts, vinegar, and ⅛ teaspoon of the pepper. Keep warm or let cool to room temperature.

Prepare a fire in a charcoal grill or preheat a gas grill or broiler to medium-high or 400°F. Position the cooking rack 4–6 inches from the heat source.

Rub the tuna steaks with the remaining 1 teaspoon oil. Sprinkle with the remaining ¼ teaspoon salt and the remaining ⅛ teaspoon pepper. Grill or broil, turning once, until the fish is opaque throughout when tested with the tip of a knife and shows only a small amount of pink in the center, 3–4 minutes per side. Transfer to warmed individual plates and serve topped with the salsa.

1 tablespoon pine nuts

3 teaspoons olive oil

¼ yellow onion, vertically sliced

2 cloves garlic, thinly sliced

½ cup chopped yellow bell pepper (1-inch chunks)

½ cup chopped red bell pepper (1-inch chunks)

½ cup water

½ teaspoon salt

2 tablespoons chopped fresh parsley

½ teaspoon sherry vinegar or red wine vinegar

¼ teaspoon freshly ground pepper

4 tuna steaks, each 5 oz and about 1½ inches thick

NUTRIENT ANALYSIS FOR ONE SERVING

Calories 219	**Carbohydrates** 4 g	**Total Fat** 7 g
Protein 34 g	**Fiber** 1 g	**Saturated Fat** 1 g
Sodium 348 mg	**Sugars** 2 g	**Monounsaturated Fat** 4 g
Cholesterol 64 mg		**Polyunsaturated Fat** 1 g

TERIYAKI SCALLOPS

SERVES 4

¾ cup pineapple nectar or pineapple juice

⅓ cup mirin or rice wine vinegar

2 tablespoons low-sodium soy sauce

2 teaspoons dark sesame oil

1 teaspoon peeled and minced fresh ginger

1 clove garlic, minced

16 large sea scallops, about 1¼ lb total weight

1 teaspoon canola oil

A homemade teriyaki sauce—low-sodium soy sauce seasoned with pineapple, sesame, ginger, and mirin—preserves the natural sweetness of the scallops in this dish. Mirin is a sweet rice wine shelved with the Asian foods in most supermarkets.

In a glass measuring cup or small bowl, combine the pineapple nectar, mirin, soy sauce, sesame oil, ginger, and garlic. Whisk to blend.

Pour half of the pineapple nectar mixture into a small saucepan over medium-high heat and bring to a boil. Reduce the heat to medium and simmer gently until the mixture is reduced to a syrup, 20–25 minutes. (Watch to make sure the mixture doesn't burn.)

Place the scallops in a bowl with the remaining half of the pineapple nectar mixture. Let marinate for 15 minutes.

While the scallops are marinating, prepare a fire in a charcoal grill or preheat a gas grill or broiler to medium-high or 400°F. Position the cooking rack 4–6 inches from the heat source.

Drain the scallops and discard the marinade. Thread the scallops on metal or wooden skewers, and brush with the canola oil. (If you use wooden skewers, soak them in water ahead of time for about 30 minutes so they don't burn.) Grill or broil the scallops, turning frequently, until opaque throughout when tested in the center with the tip of a knife, 4–6 minutes. Brush the cooked scallops with the pineapple syrup and serve immediately.

NUTRIENT ANALYSIS FOR ONE SERVING

Calories 222	**Carbohydrates** 14 g	**Total Fat** 5 g
Protein 25 g	**Fiber** 0 g	**Saturated Fat** 1 g
Sodium 497 mg	**Sugars** 9 g	**Monounsaturated Fat** 2 g
Cholesterol 47 mg		**Polyunsaturated Fat** 2 g

THAI SHRIMP WITH RICE

DIABETIC EXCHANGES

2 starch	0 fruit	0 milk
1½ vegetable	2½ protein	½ fat

SERVES 4

Crisp sugar snap peas and sweet fresh shrimp are paired in this dish with classic Thai seasonings: garlic, chile, basil, and lime. If you can't find prepared chile-garlic sauce (or purée), substitute ½ teaspoon red pepper flakes and 1 more clove of garlic, minced.

In a saucepan, combine the rice and water. Bring to a boil over medium-high heat. Reduce the heat to low, cover, and simmer until the water is absorbed and the rice is tender, about 45 minutes. Transfer to a large bowl and keep warm.

While the rice is cooking, in a large nonstick frying pan, heat the sesame oil over medium-high heat. Add the shrimp, garlic, and chile-garlic sauce. Toss and stir until the mixture is sizzling, about 2 minutes. Add the sugar snap peas and continue to toss and stir until the shrimp are opaque and the peas are tender-crisp, 3–4 minutes.

In a small bowl, combine the broth, soy sauce, and cornstarch and stir to mix well. Add the broth mixture to the shrimp mixture and toss until the sauce thickens, about 1 minute. Divide the cooked rice among individual plates and top with the shrimp mixture. Drizzle with the lime juice and garnish with the basil, if desired.

⅔ cup long-grain brown rice

1½ cups water

1 teaspoon dark sesame oil

¾ lb large shrimp, peeled and deveined

3 cloves garlic, minced

2 teaspoons chile-garlic sauce

½ lb small sugar snap peas, trimmed

½ cup fat-free, no-salt-added chicken broth

1 tablespoon low-sodium soy sauce

2 teaspoons cornstarch

2 tablespoons fresh lime juice

2 tablespoons chopped fresh basil (optional)

NUTRIENT ANALYSIS FOR ONE SERVING

Calories 295	**Carbohydrates** 40 g	**Total Fat** 4 g
Protein 24 g	**Fiber** 5 g	**Saturated Fat** 1 g
Sodium 471 mg	**Sugars** 6 g	**Monounsaturated Fat** 1 g
Cholesterol 129 mg		**Polyunsaturated Fat** 1 g

6g

DIABETIC EXCHANGES

| 0 starch | 0 fruit | 0 milk |
| 1 vegetable | 4 protein | 1 fat |

CHICKEN WITH CARAMELIZED ONIONS

SERVES 4

4 teaspoons olive oil or canola oil

1 large yellow or white onion, about 8 oz, halved vertically and cut into thin slivers

½ teaspoon salt

⅓ cup chicken stock or fat-free, no salt added chicken broth

½ tablespoon balsamic vinegar

1 teaspoon whole-grain mustard

¼ teaspoon freshly ground pepper

4 skinless, boneless chicken breasts, 4 oz each

1½ tablespoons chopped fresh thyme, plus several sprigs for garnish (optional)

As onions cook slowly, their natural sharpness fades. After enough slow cooking, the onions caramelize—that is, they become dark, sweet, and rich with a texture like that of jam.

In a large nonstick frying pan, heat 3 teaspoons of the oil over medium-low heat. Add the onion and cook, stirring frequently, until the onion is golden brown, about 20 minutes. (Do not let the onion burn.) Stir in ¼ teaspoon of the salt.

In a small saucepan over medium-low heat, combine the stock, vinegar, and mustard and whisk to blend. Add the onion and ⅛ teaspoon of the pepper and cook until the liquid is reduced by half, 4–5 minutes. Remove from the heat and keep warm.

Place the chicken breasts between 2 sheets of heavy-duty plastic wrap. With a meat mallet or rolling pin, pound the breasts to an even ¼-inch thickness. Sprinkle the pounded chicken with the remaining ¼ teaspoon salt and the remaining ⅛ teaspoon pepper. Place the chopped thyme in a shallow dish. Dredge the chicken in the thyme, pressing to make the leaves stick.

In the same large nonstick pan used for the onion, heat the remaining 1 teaspoon oil over medium-high heat. Add the chicken and cook, turning once, until opaque throughout, about 2–3 minutes per side.

To serve, place the chicken on individual plates and top with the onion sauce. Garnish with a sprig of thyme, if desired.

NUTRIENT ANALYSIS FOR ONE SERVING

Calories 191	**Carbohydrates** 6 g	**Total Fat** 6 g
Protein 27 g	**Fiber** 1 g	**Saturated Fat** 1 g
Sodium 390 mg	**Sugars** 4 g	**Monounsaturated Fat** 4 g
Cholesterol 66 mg		**Polyunsaturated Fat** 1 g

CHICKEN BREASTS STUFFED WITH TOMATO & BASIL

SERVES 4

1 oz fresh mozzarella cheese, diced

4 large basil leaves, chopped

1 small plum (Roma) tomato, seeded and finely chopped (about ½ cup)

½ teaspoon salt

4 skinless, boneless chicken breasts, 4 oz each

3 tablespoons all-purpose flour

¼ teaspoon paprika

¼ teaspoon freshly ground pepper

1 tablespoon olive oil or canola oil

Simply slice pockets into chicken breasts to add a tasty stuffing. Here, the chicken breasts are filled with chopped tomatoes, mozzarella, and fresh basil. Try whole-grain bread crumbs with chopped nuts and parsley for another healthy stuffing.

In a small bowl, combine the mozzarella cheese, chopped basil, tomato, and ¼ teaspoon of the salt.

Place 1 chicken breast on a cutting board and hold it flat with your hand. Using a small, sharp knife, cut a horizontal slice in the side of the breast to make a pocket as large as you can without cutting through the other side. Repeat with the remaining chicken breasts. Spoon one-fourth of the cheese-tomato mixture into each pocket and pin the pocket closed with a toothpick.

In a shallow bowl, combine the flour, paprika, pepper, and the remaining ¼ teaspoon salt. Dredge the stuffed chicken breasts in the flour mixture to coat well.

In a large frying pan, heat the oil over medium-high heat. Add the stuffed chicken breasts and cook, turning once, until opaque throughout and tender, 4–5 minutes per side. Transfer to a warmed serving platter. Remove the toothpicks and serve immediately.

NUTRIENT ANALYSIS FOR ONE SERVING

Calories 201	**Carbohydrates** 6 g	**Total Fat** 6 g
Protein 28 g	**Fiber** 0 g	**Saturated Fat** 2 g
Sodium 396 mg	**Sugars** 1 g	**Monounsaturated Fat** 3 g
Cholesterol 71 mg		**Polyunsaturated Fat** 1 g

TURKEY & VEGETABLE MEATLOAF

CARB COUNT 14g

DIABETIC EXCHANGES
½ starch   0 fruit   0 milk
½ vegetable   3 protein   0 fat

SERVES 6

Diced and grated fresh vegetables and a sprinkling of oats help keep this meatloaf deliciously moist. Accompanied by Mashed Sweet Potatoes (page 107) and steamed green beans, it's comfort food at its best. Slice any leftovers for meatloaf sandwiches.

Preheat the oven to 350°F.

In a large bowl, combine the oats and chicken broth. Let stand until most of the liquid is absorbed, 20–25 minutes. Add the ground turkey, onion, carrot, mushrooms, tomato paste, thyme, sage, egg whites, salt, and pepper. Mix with a large spoon or by hand until well blended.

Place the turkey mixture in a nonstick 9-by-5-inch loaf pan, pressing down gently to fit. Bake until no longer pink inside and an instant-read thermometer inserted in the center reads 160°F, 50–55 minutes. Let stand for 15 minutes before slicing.

1 cup old-fashioned rolled oats

½ cup fat-free, no-salt-added chicken broth

1¼ lb lean ground (minced) turkey

½ onion, diced or coarsely chopped (about ½ cup)

½ large carrot, coarsely grated, about ½ cup

2 cups diced cremini or button mushrooms

¼ cup tomato paste

1 tablespoon chopped fresh thyme or 1 teaspoon dried thyme

1 tablespoon chopped fresh sage or 1 teaspoon ground dried sage

2 egg whites, lightly beaten

½ teaspoon salt

½ teaspoon freshly ground pepper

NUTRIENT ANALYSIS FOR ONE SERVING

Calories 222	**Carbohydrates** 14 g	**Total Fat** 8 g
Protein 25 g	**Fiber** 3 g	**Saturated Fat** 2 g
Sodium 329 mg	**Sugars** 2 g	**Monounsaturated Fat** 5 g
Cholesterol 59 mg		**Polyunsaturated Fat** 1 g

BRAISED CHICKEN WITH TOMATOES & OLIVES

CARB COUNT 14g

SERVES 4

DIABETIC EXCHANGES

½ starch	0 fruit	0 milk
2 vegetable	3½ protein	½ fat

Green olives, capers, oregano, and other seasonings are combined with a bit of Marsala, a sweet wine from Sicily, to give this savory chicken dish a Mediterranean character. For a complete meal, pair it with whole-grain bread and a salad.

In a shallow bowl, combine the flour, oregano, black pepper, and red pepper flakes. Dredge the chicken pieces in the flour mixture.

In a large saucepan or Dutch oven coated generously with cooking spray, heat the olive oil over medium-high heat. Add the chicken and cook until browned on all sides, about 5 minutes. Transfer the chicken to a platter. Add the onion to the pan and sauté until it begins to soften and brown, about 4 minutes. Add the tomatoes and sauté for 2 minutes. Stir in the stock and Marsala, stirring with a wooden spoon to scrape up any browned bits. Return the chicken to the pan. Bring to a boil, reduce the heat to low, cover, and simmer, stirring occasionally, until the chicken is tender, 45–50 minutes. Stir in the chopped parsley, olives, capers, and salt.

To serve, place 1 chicken breast piece and 1 chicken thigh in warmed individual bowls. Top with the onion mixture and garnish with a sprig of parsley, if desired.

¼ cup all-purpose flour

1 teaspoon dried oregano

¼ teaspoon freshly ground black pepper

⅛ teaspoon red pepper flakes

2 small bone-in chicken breast halves, about 6 oz each, skinned and cut in half crosswise

4 bone-in chicken thighs, about 6 oz each, skinned

Cooking spray

1½ teaspoons olive oil

1 large yellow or white onion, sliced vertically (about 2 cups)

2 small plum (Roma) tomatoes, diced (about 1 cup)

½ cup chicken stock or fat-free, no-salt-added chicken broth

½ cup Marsala or dry red wine

¼ cup chopped fresh parsley, plus sprigs for garnish (optional)

¼ cup small pitted green olives, halved

1 tablespoon capers, rinsed

⅛ teaspoon salt

NUTRIENT ANALYSIS FOR ONE SERVING

Calories 221	Carbohydrates 14 g	Total Fat 7 g
Protein 25 g	Fiber 2 g	Saturated Fat 2 g
Sodium 356 mg	Sugars 5 g	Monounsaturated Fat 3 g
Cholesterol 67 mg		Polyunsaturated Fat 1 g

PAN-SEARED DUCK BREAST WITH ORANGE SAUCE

SERVES 4

2 teaspoons grated orange zest

¾ cup fresh orange juice

4 skinless, boneless duck or chicken breasts, about 4 oz each

¼ teaspoon salt, plus ⅛ teaspoon

¼ teaspoon freshly ground pepper

1 tablespoon olive oil or canola oil

½ cup chicken stock or fat-free, no-salt-added chicken broth

1 tablespoon chopped fresh chives

1 tablespoon chopped fresh parsley

1 teaspoon chopped fresh tarragon

Skinless chicken breast is a mainstay for healthy eaters, but skinless duck breast is actually leaner—and more flavorful. Duck has also become easier to find in supermarkets. Check the weights and divide the breasts if they are too large.

In a large shallow nonaluminum container or a lock-top plastic bag, combine the orange zest and ½ cup of the orange juice. Add the duck and turn to coat both sides. Cover or seal the container and refrigerate, turning occasionally, for 30 minutes. Remove the duck from the marinade and pat dry with paper towels. Discard the marinade. Sprinkle the duck with ¼ teaspoon of the salt and ⅛ teaspoon of the pepper.

In a large nonstick frying pan, heat the oil over medium heat. Add the duck and cook, turning once, until medium-well done, with only a hint of pink in the center, about 6 minutes per side. Transfer to a platter and let stand for 5 minutes.

Add the chicken stock and the remaining ¼ cup orange juice to the frying pan over medium-high heat and deglaze the pan, stirring with a wooden spoon to scrape up any browned bits. Bring to a boil, reduce the heat to low, and simmer until the mixture is reduced by one-third, 3–4 minutes. Remove from the heat and stir in the chives, parsley, tarragon, the remaining ⅛ teaspoon salt, and the remaining ⅛ teaspoon pepper.

To serve, slice each duck breast on the diagonal into thin slices. Fan the slices on a warmed serving platter and top with the sauce.

NUTRIENT ANALYSIS FOR ONE SERVING

Calories 208	**Carbohydrates** 4 g	**Total Fat** 6 g
Protein 32 g	**Fiber** 0 g	**Saturated Fat** 1 g
Sodium 353 mg	**Sugars** 3 g	**Monounsaturated Fat** 3 g
Cholesterol 162 mg		**Polyunsaturated Fat** 1 g

SEARED SIRLOIN WITH SWEET POTATO RAGOUT

CARB COUNT 22g

DIABETIC EXCHANGES
1 starch	0 fruit	0 milk
1 vegetable	3½ protein	1½ fat

SERVES 4

Rich with the flavors of garlic and thyme, this dish takes only minutes to prepare yet is elegant enough to serve to guests. Asparagus with Shallots & Blue Cheese (page 46) is an excellent complement to this hearty-but-light main course.

Combine the broth and sweet potatoes in a large deep frying pan. Bring to a simmer over medium heat, cover, and cook for 8 minutes. Add the sliced mushrooms, shallots, garlic, mustard, thyme, and ¼ teaspoon of the pepper. Cook, stirring frequently, until the vegetables are tender and the sauce is slightly reduced, about 5 minutes. Remove from the heat and keep warm while preparing the steak.

Heat a large nonstick frying pan over medium-high heat until hot. Place the steak in the frying pan and sprinkle with the salt and the remaining ¼ teaspoon pepper. Cook, turning once, until browned, 4 minutes per side. Cut into the center to check for doneness. Transfer the steak to a carving board.

Cut the steak across the grain into thin slices. Spoon the sweet potato ragout onto warmed individual plates; top with the sliced steak. Garnish with thyme sprigs, if desired, and serve immediately.

¾ cup fat-free, no-salt-added beef broth

2 sweet potatoes, about 1 lb total weight, cut into ½-inch cubes

½ lb sliced cremini or button mushrooms, brushed clean and sliced, or packaged sliced mixed fresh mushrooms such as oyster, cremini, and shiitake

¼ cup finely chopped shallots

2 cloves garlic, minced

1½ tablespoons Dijon or hot French Dijon mustard

1½ tablespoons chopped fresh thyme, plus several thyme sprigs for garnish (optional)

½ teaspoon freshly ground pepper

1 lb beef top sirloin steak, 1 inch thick and trimmed of visible fat

¼ teaspoon salt

NUTRIENT ANALYSIS FOR ONE SERVING

Calories 289	**Carbohydrates** 22 g	**Total Fat** 9 g
Protein 30 g	**Fiber** 4 g	**Saturated Fat** 3 g
Sodium 385 mg	**Sugars** 7 g	**Monounsaturated Fat** 4 g
Cholesterol 74 mg		**Polyunsaturated Fat** 1 g

PORK LOIN WITH APPLES

SERVES 4

1½ teaspoons paprika

1½ teaspoons dried sage or thyme

½ teaspoon salt

¼ teaspoon freshly ground pepper

½ teaspoon ground allspice

4 boneless center-cut pork loin chops, each about 4 oz and ½ inch thick, trimmed of visible fat

3 Granny Smith apples, peeled, cored, and cut into ¼-inch slices

⅓ cup chopped shallots or sweet onion

½ cup unsweetened apple juice

2 teaspoons cider vinegar

1 tablespoon chopped fresh sage or thyme (optional)

Surprisingly lean, these pork loin chops can easily claim a spot on a heart-healthy menu. Granny Smith apples make an ideal partner for the pork, but feel free to use Fuji, Gala, or other crisp varieties. Serve with steamed green beans or broccoli.

Prepare a fire in a charcoal grill or preheat a gas grill or broiler to medium-high or 400°F. Position the cooking rack 4–6 inches from the heat source.

In a small bowl, combine the paprika, dried sage, salt, pepper, and ¼ teaspoon of the allspice. Sprinkle the mixture over both sides of the pork chops. Grill or broil, turning once, until the pork is browned on both sides and is no longer pink on the inside, about 5 minutes per side.

Meanwhile, in a large nonstick frying pan over high heat, combine the apples, shallots, apple juice, vinegar, and the remaining ¼ teaspoon allspice. Bring to a boil, reduce the heat to medium, and cook, stirring occasionally, until the apples are tender and the sauce is slightly reduced, 10–12 minutes. Transfer the pork chops to individual plates, top with the sauce, and garnish with the fresh sage, if desired.

NUTRIENT ANALYSIS FOR ONE SERVING

Calories 268	Carbohydrates 24 g	Total Fat 9 g
Protein 25 g	Fiber 2 g	Saturated Fat 3 g
Sodium 344 mg	Sugars 15 g	Monounsaturated Fat 4 g
Cholesterol 62 mg		Polyunsaturated Fat 1 g

VEAL PICCATA

SERVES 4

Often overlooked, veal is among the leanest meats. It is easy to cook, especially when purchased in thin cutlets. The Italian specialty called *piccata* features capers, garlic, lemon zest, and parsley. Serve it with Polenta with Garlic & Basil (page 104).

Combine the flour, salt, and pepper in a plastic or paper bag. Add the veal cutlets to the bag one at a time, shaking to coat.

In a large nonstick frying pan, heat 1 teaspoon of the olive oil over medium-high heat. Add half of the veal cutlets and cook, turning once, until lightly browned on both sides, about 2 minutes per side. Transfer to a plate and set aside. Repeat with the remaining 1 teaspoon olive oil and the remaining veal cutlets.

In the same frying pan over medium heat, add half of the garlic and cook until fragrant, about 30 seconds. Add the broth and lemon juice and simmer, stirring once, until the sauce is slightly reduced, 3–4 minutes.

In a small bowl, combine the parsley, capers, lemon zest, and the remaining garlic. Stir the parsley mixture into the sauce. Return the veal to the frying pan and warm, turning once, just until heated through.

2 tablespoons all-purpose flour

½ teaspoon salt

¼ teaspoon freshly ground pepper

1 lb veal cutlets (scaloppine), cut ¼ inch thick

2 teaspoons olive oil

2 cloves garlic, minced

½ cup fat-free, no-salt-added chicken broth

1 tablespoon fresh lemon juice

3 tablespoons chopped fresh parsley

1 tablespoon capers, rinsed

½ teaspoon grated lemon zest

NUTRIENT ANALYSIS FOR ONE SERVING

Calories 163	Carbohydrates 4 g	Total Fat 4 g
Protein 26 g	Fiber 0 g	Saturated Fat 1 g
Sodium 305 mg	Sugars 0 g	Monounsaturated Fat 2 g
Cholesterol 88 mg		Polyunsaturated Fat 0 g

SZECHUAN PORK STIR-FRY

SERVES 4

1 pork tenderloin, about 1 lb, trimmed of visible fat

1 teaspoon crushed Szechuan peppercorns or red pepper flakes

3 cloves garlic, minced

2 teaspoons peeled and minced fresh ginger or 1 teaspoon ground ginger

1 teaspoon canola oil

1 red bell pepper, cut into short, thin strips

2 cups fresh snow peas, halved diagonally

½ cup diagonally sliced green onions

¼ cup hoisin sauce

2 teaspoons toasted sesame seeds

Pork tenderloin is almost as lean as skinless chicken breast. Stir-fried with spices and vegetables, it makes a complete healthy meal with unmistakable Asian flair. Take care not to overcook the pork so it stays tender and juicy.

Slice the pork crosswise into ¼-inch slices. Cut each slice in half. In a bowl, combine the pork, crushed peppercorns, garlic, and ginger and toss to coat; set aside.

Heat the canola oil in a large nonstick frying pan over medium-high heat until hot. Add the bell pepper and cook, tossing continuously, until the pepper strips start to brown, about 2 minutes. Add the snow peas and cook, tossing continuously, until slightly softened, about 1 minute. Add the pork mixture and cook, tossing continuously, until the mixture begins to thicken, about 2 minutes. Add the green onions and hoisin sauce and cook, tossing continuously, until the pork is no longer pink in the center, 2–3 minutes. Transfer to a serving dish and garnish with the sesame seeds. Serve immediately.

NUTRIENT ANALYSIS FOR ONE SERVING

Calories 278	Carbohydrates 20 g	Total Fat 9 g
Protein 28 g	Fiber 4 g	Saturated Fat 3 g
Sodium 388 mg	Sugars 5 g	Monounsaturated Fat 4 g
Cholesterol 78 mg		Polyunsaturated Fat 2 g

LEEK & RED PEPPER FRITTATA

SERVES 4

1½ teaspoons olive oil or canola oil

1 large leek, thinly sliced (about 2 cups)

1 small potato, peeled and grated

½ cup diced red bell pepper

¼ teaspoon salt

2 whole eggs plus 3 egg whites

¼ cup nonfat milk

4 large basil leaves, chopped

¼ teaspoon freshly ground pepper

⅛ teaspoon freshly grated nutmeg

¼ cup grated Parmesan cheese

Lightened with egg whites and nonfat milk, this easy low-fat baked omelette, or frittata, is enjoyable at any meal. You can replace the leek and red pepper with other vegetables, or add chopped smoked turkey or other cooked lean meat.

Preheat the broiler.

In a large nonstick frying pan with an ovenproof handle, heat the oil over medium heat. Add the sliced leek and grated potato and sauté until tender, 8–10 minutes. Stir in the diced bell pepper and ⅛ teaspoon of the salt and cook for 2 minutes. Spread the vegetables evenly in the pan.

In a bowl, whisk together the whole eggs and egg whites. Stir in the milk, basil, the remaining ⅛ teaspoon salt, pepper, and nutmeg. Pour the egg mixture into the pan with the vegetables and sprinkle the cheese evenly over the top. Cook until slightly set, about 2 minutes.

Carefully place the pan under the broiler and broil until the frittata is brown and puffy and completely set, about 3 minutes. Gently slide onto a warmed serving platter and cut into wedges. Serve immediately.

NUTRIENT ANALYSIS FOR ONE SERVING

Calories 137	Carbohydrates 17 g	Total Fat 5 g
Protein 8 g	Fiber 2 g	Saturated Fat 1 g
Sodium 239 mg	Sugars 4 g	Monounsaturated Fat 2 g
Cholesterol 107 mg		Polyunsaturated Fat 1 g

ROTINI WITH ROASTED VEGETABLES

CARB COUNT 58g

DIABETIC EXCHANGES

| 3 starch | 0 fruit | 0 milk |
| 2 vegetable | 2 protein | 2 fat |

SERVES 4

Roasting vegetables gives them a smoky sweetness that's irresistible with pastas. To make the most nutritious version of this dish, use 100-percent whole-wheat pasta. But if you want a milder flavor, look for 50-percent whole-wheat pasta.

Preheat the oven to 400°F.

Arrange the chunks of zucchini, bell pepper, and onion on a nonstick baking sheet. Drizzle with 2 tablespoons of the olive oil. Sprinkle with ¼ teaspoon of the salt and ⅛ teaspoon of the pepper. Toss gently to mix. Add the unpeeled garlic cloves to the baking sheet and roast until the vegetables are nearly tender and beginning to brown, 20–25 minutes. Add the tomatoes and continue to roast for 10 minutes longer.

While the tomatoes are roasting, bring a large pot three-fourths full of water to a boil. Add the rotini and cook until al dente, 10–12 minutes, or according to package directions. Drain the pasta thoroughly, transfer to a large bowl, and toss with the remaining 1 tablespoon olive oil.

Peel the roasted garlic and mash with a fork. Stir the garlic into the pasta. Stir the remaining roasted vegetables into the pasta. Add the parsley, chopped basil, thyme, the remaining ¼ teaspoon salt, and the remaining ⅛ teaspoon pepper. Toss gently to mix.

To serve, divide the pasta mixture evenly among shallow, warmed bowls. Using a vegetable peeler, cut a curl or two of Parmesan cheese to top each serving. Garnish with a leaf of basil, if desired.

2 small zucchini, about ½ lb total weight, cut into 1-inch chunks

2 yellow bell peppers, about ½ lb total weight, seeded and cut into 1-inch chunks

½ onion, cut into 1-inch chunks

3 tablespoons olive oil

½ teaspoon salt

¼ teaspoon freshly ground pepper

10 cloves garlic, unpeeled

8 plum (Roma) tomatoes, about 1 lb total weight, seeded and coarsely chopped

½ lb whole-wheat or 50-percent whole-wheat rotini or other dry pasta

3 tablespoons chopped fresh parsley

3 tablespoons chopped fresh basil, plus 4 leaves for garnish (optional)

½ tablespoon chopped fresh thyme

1-oz chunk Parmesan cheese

NUTRIENT ANALYSIS FOR ONE SERVING

Calories 380	Carbohydrates 58 g	Total Fat 13 g
Protein 14 g	Fiber 5 g	Saturated Fat 3 g
Sodium 409 mg	Sugars 9 g	Monounsaturated Fat 8 g
Cholesterol 4 mg		Polyunsaturated Fat 2 g

WINTER SQUASH TART

DIABETIC EXCHANGES

1½ starch	0 fruit	0 milk
1 vegetable	1 protein	1½ fat

SERVES 4

Flavorful poblano chiles add a touch of spiciness to this healthful tart. Use red, green, or yellow bell peppers in place of the chiles, if you like, and add a pinch of cayenne pepper.

Preheat the broiler. Flatten the poblano chile halves with your hand. Broil the chile until the skin blackens, 5–6 minutes. Place the chile in a small bowl, cover with plastic wrap, and let stand until the skin loosens, about 15 minutes. Peel and discard the skin. Slice the chile into thin strips.

In a large bowl, combine the whole-wheat and all-purpose flours, cornmeal, baking powder, and ⅛ teaspoon of the salt. Add ¼ cup of the water and the oil to the flour mixture and stir until blended. Turn the dough out onto a floured surface and knead 4 or 5 times. Press the dough into a 4-inch round, place between sheets of plastic wrap, and refrigerate for 15 minutes. Roll the dough, still covered, into a 10-inch round. Transfer the round to the freezer and chill for 5 minutes or until the plastic wrap can be easily removed.

Preheat the oven to 375°F. Press the rolled crust into a 9-inch tart pan or quiche pan coated with cooking spray, pinching the edges to fit. Bake the crust until brown, about 8 minutes. Cool on a wire rack.

Place the squash in a microwave steamer with the remaining ¼ cup water. Cover and microwave on high until tender, 4–5 minutes. Drain. Spoon the squash into the crust and spread evenly. Arrange the chile strips on top. In a bowl, whisk together the egg, egg whites, milk, oregano, the remaining ¼ teaspoon salt, and pepper. Pour the egg mixture over the vegetables in the crust. Sprinkle with the cheese. Bake until fully set, 20–25 minutes.

1 poblano chile, about 4 oz, halved and seeded

½ cup whole-wheat flour

⅓ cup all-purpose flour

¼ cup stone-ground cornmeal

1 teaspoon baking powder

⅛ teaspoon salt, plus ¼ teaspoon

½ cup water

1½ tablespoons olive oil or canola oil

Cooking spray

1½ cups chopped, peeled butternut or acorn squash

1 whole egg plus 2 egg whites

½ cup nonfat milk

2 tablespoons chopped fresh oregano or ¾ teaspoon dried oregano

¼ teaspoon freshly ground pepper

2 tablespoons shredded Monterey Jack cheese

NUTRIENT ANALYSIS FOR ONE SERVING

Calories 244	**Carbohydrates** 35 g	**Total Fat** 8 g
Protein 10 g	**Fiber** 5 g	**Saturated Fat** 2 g
Sodium 499 mg	**Sugars** 4 g	**Monounsaturated Fat** 5 g
Cholesterol 79 mg		**Polyunsaturated Fat** 1 g

SPINACH & GARLIC LASAGNE

SERVES 6

1 tablespoon olive oil or canola oil

15 cloves garlic, thinly sliced

10 cups baby spinach leaves

¼ teaspoon salt

2 eggs, lightly beaten

1 cup low-fat cottage cheese

1 cup part-skim ricotta cheese

3 tablespoons finely chopped toasted walnuts (page 138)

3 tablespoons chopped fresh parsley

3 tablespoons chopped fresh chives

4 tablespoons chopped fresh basil

2 cups nonfat milk

¼ cup all-purpose flour

¼ teaspoon pepper

Cooking spray

9 cooked whole-wheat lasagne noodles

1 large plum (Roma) tomato, about 4 oz, thinly sliced

¼ cup grated Parmesan cheese

Preheat the oven to 375°F. In a large frying pan, heat ½ tablespoon of the oil over medium heat. Add the garlic and sauté until lightly browned, 1–2 minutes. Transfer the garlic to a small plate. Add half of the spinach to the pan. Sauté until the spinach wilts, 4–5 minutes. Stir in ⅛ teaspoon of the salt and transfer the cooked spinach to a large bowl. Add the remaining ½ tablespoon oil and spinach to the pan. Repeat, sautéing until the spinach wilts. Stir in the remaining ⅛ teaspoon salt; transfer the spinach to the same bowl. When the spinach has cooled, add the eggs, cottage cheese, half of the garlic, the ricotta, toasted walnuts, parsley, chives, and 1 tablespoon of the basil. Toss gently to mix well. Set aside.

In a saucepan over medium heat, combine the milk, flour, and remaining garlic and whisk until blended. Cook, stirring constantly, until thickened, 8–10 minutes. Remove from heat and stir in the remaining 3 tablespoons basil and the pepper.

Lightly coat a 9-by-13-inch baking dish with cooking spray. Spread ½ cup of the garlic sauce in the dish. Arrange 3 noodles lengthwise over the sauce and spread half of the spinach-cheese mixture on top. Top with another ½ cup sauce. Repeat with the remaining noodles, the remaining spinach-cheese mixture, and another ½ cup sauce, beginning and ending with noodles. Spread the remaining sauce over the noodles. Arrange the tomato slices on the coated noodles and sprinkle with the Parmesan.

Cover with aluminum foil and bake for 15 minutes. Uncover and continue to bake until the noodles are tender and the sauce is bubbly, about 20 minutes longer. Let stand for 15 minutes before serving.

NUTRIENT ANALYSIS FOR ONE SERVING

Calories 350	Carbohydrates 39 g	Total Fat 12 g
Protein 24 g	**Fiber** 5 g	**Saturated Fat** 4 g
Sodium 493 mg	**Sugars** 8 g	**Monounsaturated Fat** 4 g
Cholesterol 90 mg		**Polyunsaturated Fat** 3 g

VEGETABLE GUMBO

SERVES 4

Sprinklings of three kinds of pepper give this contemporary New Orleans gumbo an alluring spiciness. Filé powder—a mild seasoning made of sassafras leaves—is a traditional thickener for gumbos and other stews, but you can leave it out.

In a saucepan, combine the rice, water, and ¼ teaspoon of the salt. Bring to a boil. Reduce the heat to low, cover, and simmer until the water is absorbed and the rice is tender, about 45 minutes. Transfer to a large bowl and keep warm.

While the rice is cooking, in a large heavy saucepan, heat the canola oil over medium heat. Add the flour and cook, stirring often, until the flour is golden brown, about 7 minutes. Add the bell pepper, onion, carrots, and garlic and stir to mix well. Cover, raise the heat to high, and cook for 3 minutes. Uncover and stir in the broth, thyme, paprika, white pepper, black pepper, cayenne, and the remaining ¼ teaspoon salt. Cover and bring to a boil over high heat. Reduce the heat to medium-low and simmer, covered, until the vegetables are tender, about 15 minutes. Stir in the okra and continue to simmer, covered, 5 minutes longer. Stir in the filé powder, if desired.

Divide the rice among individual bowls. Top each serving with the gumbo and sprinkle with the parsley.

1 cup brown rice

2 cups water

½ teaspoon salt

1 tablespoon canola oil

2 tablespoons all-purpose flour

1 large green or red bell pepper, coarsely chopped

1 yellow onion, coarsely chopped

1½ cups chopped or sliced carrots

4 cloves garlic, minced

3 cups fat-free, no-salt-added chicken or vegetable broth

1 tablespoon chopped fresh thyme or 1 teaspoon dried thyme

1 teaspoon paprika

¼ teaspoon ground white pepper

¼ teaspoon freshly ground black pepper

⅛ teaspoon cayenne pepper

1 package frozen precut okra, thawed, about 2 cups

1 teaspoon filé powder (optional)

¼ cup chopped fresh parsley

NUTRIENT ANALYSIS FOR ONE SERVING

Calories 307	Carbohydrates 54 g	Total Fat 5 g
Protein 11 g	Fiber 7 g	Saturated Fat 1 g
Sodium 459 mg	Sugars 8 g	Monounsaturated Fat 3 g
Cholesterol 0 mg		Polyunsaturated Fat 2 g

41g

DIABETIC EXCHANGES

2½ starch	0 fruit	0 milk
1 vegetable	2 protein	1 fat

BLACK BEAN TOSTADAS WITH SWEET ONIONS

SERVES 4

2 teaspoons canola oil

1 large Vidalia, Walla Walla, Maui, or other sweet onion, thinly sliced and separated into rings

4 corn tortillas, 6–7 inches in diameter

One 15-oz can no-salt-added black beans, rinsed and drained

½ cup fat-free, no-salt-added vegetable or chicken broth

4 plum (Roma) tomatoes, diced

2 jalapeño chiles, seeded and minced

3 cloves garlic, thinly sliced

1 teaspoon ground cumin

½ teaspoon salt

½ cup crumbled farmer's cheese

¼ cup chopped fresh cilantro

Naturally high in protein and in heart-healthy fiber and folate, black beans form the centerpiece of this nutrient-rich and tasty dish. You can substitute ½ cup dried black beans for the canned beans. (For tips on cooking dried beans, see page 135.)

Preheat the oven to 400°F.

In a large nonstick frying pan, heat 1 teaspoon of the canola oil over medium-high heat and add the onion rings. Cover and cook until golden brown, about 4 minutes. Uncover and stir well. Reduce the heat to medium and continue cooking until the onion is soft and deep golden brown, 6–8 minutes longer. Set aside and keep warm.

Place the tortillas on a baking sheet and brush them with the remaining 1 teaspoon oil. Bake for 5 minutes. Turn the tortillas over and continue baking until crisp, 7–8 minutes. Remove from the heat and set aside.

In a saucepan over medium heat, combine the beans, broth, tomatoes, jalapeños, garlic, cumin, and salt. Simmer, uncovered, until most of the liquid is absorbed, about 10 minutes. Place the baked tortillas on individual plates and top with the bean mixture, onion, cheese, and cilantro, dividing evenly. Serve immediately.

NUTRIENT ANALYSIS FOR ONE SERVING

Calories 278	**Carbohydrates** 41 g	**Total Fat** 8 g
Protein 13 g	**Fiber** 8 g	**Saturated Fat** 3 g
Sodium 499 mg	**Sugars** 9 g	**Monounsaturated Fat** 3 g
Cholesterol 13 mg		**Polyunsaturated Fat** 1 g

LO MEIN NOODLES WITH SPINACH & TOFU

SERVES 4

CARB COUNT **55**g

DIABETIC EXCHANGES

2½ starch   0 fruit   ½ other carbs
1 vegetable   2½ protein   1½ fat

If you like Asian food, you will appreciate the complex mix of flavors in this soup. Preparing the ingredients takes a little time, but the soup comes together quickly. Look for the noodles and sesame oil in the Asian foods section of your supermarket.

In a saucepan, combine the noodles and water. Bring to a boil over medium-high heat. Reduce the heat to low, cover, and simmer until the noodles are tender but still slightly firm, about 12 minutes. Drain.

While the noodles are cooking, heat the sesame oil in a large, deep frying pan over medium heat. Add the garlic and ginger and sauté until fragrant, about 2 minutes. Add the broth, carrot, and teriyaki sauce and bring to a simmer. Reduce the heat to low and simmer until the carrot is tender, about 2 minutes. Stir in the spinach and cook until wilted, about 1 minute. Stir in the tofu and heat through. Add the cooked noodles and toss well to mix. Transfer the soup to shallow serving bowls and top with the cilantro and chopped peanuts.

½ lb wide lo mein or udon noodles

2 cups water

2 teaspoons dark sesame oil

4 cloves garlic, minced

2 teaspoons peeled and minced fresh ginger

2 cups fat-free, no-salt-added chicken or vegetable broth

1 carrot, thinly sliced or cut into matchsticks

⅓ cup low-sodium teriyaki sauce

5 cups packed baby spinach or torn spinach leaves

10–11 oz extra-firm tofu, drained, cut into 1-inch cubes

¼ cup chopped fresh cilantro

3 tablespoons chopped unsalted dry-roasted peanuts

NUTRIENT ANALYSIS FOR ONE SERVING

Calories 369	**Carbohydrates** 55 g	**Total Fat** 8 g
Protein 19 g	**Fiber** 3 g	**Saturated Fat** 1 g
Sodium 600 mg	**Sugars** 7 g	**Monounsaturated Fat** 3 g
Cholesterol 0 mg		**Polyunsaturated Fat** 3 g

66g

DIABETIC EXCHANGES

4 starch	0 fruit	0 milk
1 vegetable	1 protein	2½ fat

SPICY RICE & VEGETABLES WITH FRESH CILANTRO

SERVES 4

1½ cups long-grain brown rice

3 cups water

1 bay leaf

¼ teaspoon salt, plus ½ teaspoon

1 cup frozen green peas, thawed,
   or shelled English peas

1 large carrot, grated (about 1 cup)

½ cup diced red bell pepper

3 tablespoons chopped almonds

1½ tablespoons olive oil or
   canola oil

1½ teaspoons mustard seeds

1 teaspoon ground turmeric

½ teaspoon ground coriander

¼ teaspoon ground cinnamon

¼ teaspoon red pepper flakes

¼ cup chopped fresh cilantro,
   plus sprigs for garnish (optional)

Simple to prepare, this dish proves that meatless dinners can be delicious. It is based on the abundantly spiced vegetarian dishes popular in southern India. If you don't have ground turmeric on hand, simply omit it. The dish will still be rich and flavorful.

In a saucepan, combine the rice, water, bay leaf, and ¼ teaspoon of the salt. Bring to a boil over medium-high heat. Reduce the heat to low, cover tightly, and simmer for 30–35 minutes. Stir in the peas, carrot, and bell pepper. Cover again and continue cooking until the vegetables and rice are tender, 8–10 minutes longer. Discard the bay leaf.

While the rice mixture is cooking, put the almonds in a small, dry nonstick frying pan over medium-high heat. Cook, stirring often, until lightly toasted, 3–5 minutes. Set aside.

In a large frying pan, heat the oil over medium heat. Add the mustard seeds, the remaining ½ teaspoon salt, turmeric, coriander, cinnamon, and red pepper flakes. Sauté for 2 minutes. Stir in the rice mixture and cook until the mixture is heated through, 2–3 minutes. Remove from the heat and stir in the chopped cilantro.

To serve, divide the rice mixture among individual bowls. Sprinkle with the toasted almonds and garnish with a sprig of cilantro, if desired. Serve immediately.

NUTRIENT ANALYSIS FOR ONE SERVING

Calories 415	**Carbohydrates** 66 g	**Total Fat** 13 g
Protein 10 g	**Fiber** 7 g	**Saturated Fat** 1 g
Sodium 500 mg	**Sugars** 5 g	**Monounsaturated Fat** 7 g
Cholesterol 0 mg		**Polyunsaturated Fat** 3 g

WHITE BEAN STEW

CARB COUNT 31g

DIABETIC EXCHANGES
1½ starch	0 fruit	0 milk
1½ vegetable	2 protein	1½ fat

SERVES 4

In this robust stew, rosemary melds perfectly with garlic, black olives, tomatoes, and a touch of dark balsamic vinegar. You can substitute ½ cup of dried Great Northern beans for the canned beans. (For tips on cooking dried beans, see page 135.)

In a large saucepan, heat the olive oil over medium heat. Add the onion and garlic and sauté until fragrant, about 5 minutes. Add the broth and simmer until the onion is tender, about 5 minutes. Add the beans, rosemary, salt, and pepper. Simmer, uncovered, for 5 minutes. Add the tomatoes and olives and continue to simmer until the mixture is heated through, about 5 minutes longer. Remove from the heat and stir in the vinegar. Ladle into shallow serving bowls and top with the cheese.

2 teaspoons olive oil

1 yellow onion, chopped

4 cloves garlic, minced

1 cup fat-free, no-salt-added chicken or vegetable broth

One 15-oz can no-salt-added Great Northern or navy beans, rinsed and drained

1½ tablespoons chopped fresh rosemary or 1½ teaspoons dried rosemary

¼ teaspoon salt

½ teaspoon freshly ground pepper

2 large tomatoes or 4 plum (Roma) tomatoes, seeded and chopped

½ cup sliced pitted Kalamata olives

1 tablespoon balsamic vinegar

¼ cup grated Romano or Parmesan cheese

NUTRIENT ANALYSIS FOR ONE SERVING

Calories 248	**Carbohydrates** 31 g	**Total Fat** 9 g
Protein 12 g	**Fiber** 10 g	**Saturated Fat** 2 g
Sodium 520 mg	**Sugars** 7 g	**Monounsaturated Fat** 5 g
Cholesterol 7 mg		**Polyunsaturated Fat** 1 g

SIDE DISHES

Roasted Winter Vegetables, 115

22g

BLACK-EYED PEAS WITH GREENS

SERVES 6

3 teaspoons olive oil

1 oz pancetta (Italian bacon), diced, or 1 slice Canadian bacon, diced

½ yellow onion, chopped

½ celery stalk, diced

2 cloves garlic, minced

3–3½ cups thawed frozen black-eyed peas

2 cups water

¼ teaspoon salt

1½ cups coarsely chopped mustard greens

2 tablespoons chopped fresh parsley

2 teaspoons red wine vinegar

This classic Southern dish is flavored with a small amount of pancetta, or bacon. In addition to being a popular comfort food, the dish is exceptionally healthy—providing fiber, folate, and antioxidants to help protect your heart and blood vessels.

In a large saucepan, heat 1 teaspoon of the olive oil over medium heat. Add the pancetta and cook until lightly browned, 2–3 minutes. Transfer the pancetta to a plate.

Add the remaining 2 teaspoons olive oil to the pan and heat over medium heat. Add the onion and celery and sauté until the vegetables are tender, 6–8 minutes. Stir in the garlic and cook for 1 minute. Add the black-eyed peas, water, salt, and greens. Bring to a boil, reduce the heat to low, and simmer, covered, until the greens wilt and soften, 6–8 minutes. Remove from the heat and stir in the parsley and vinegar.

To serve, ladle into a warmed serving bowl and sprinkle with the browned pancetta. Serve immediately.

NUTRIENT ANALYSIS FOR ONE SERVING

Calories 146	**Carbohydrates** 22 g	**Total Fat** 3 g
Protein 8 g	**Fiber** 6 g	**Saturated Fat** 1 g
Sodium 129 mg	**Sugars** 4 g	**Monounsaturated Fat** 2 g
Cholesterol 1 mg		**Polyunsaturated Fat** <1 g

HERBED CHICKPEA RICE

SERVES 6

½ cup long-grain brown rice

1 cup water

1 bay leaf

⅛ teaspoon salt, plus ¼ teaspoon

One 15-oz can no-salt-added chickpeas (garbanzo beans), rinsed and drained

¼ teaspoon grated lemon zest

1 tablespoon fresh lemon juice

2 teaspoons olive oil

2 tablespoons chopped fresh parsley

2 tablespoons chopped fresh basil

1 tablespoon chopped fresh thyme

¼ teaspoon freshly ground pepper

Lemon flavors enliven this tasty, fiber-rich side dish. For a colorful vegetarian meal, pair it with Beet & Spinach Salad (page 50). You can substitute ⅔ cup dried white beans for the canned beans. (For tips on cooking dried beans, see page 135.)

In a large saucepan, combine the rice, water, bay leaf, and ⅛ teaspoon of the salt over high heat. Bring the mixture to a boil. Reduce the heat to low, cover, and simmer until the rice is tender, about 45 minutes. Add the chickpeas and continue cooking until the chickpeas are heated through, 3–4 minutes. Remove from the heat and stir in the lemon zest, the remaining ¼ teaspoon salt, the lemon juice, olive oil, parsley, basil, thyme, and pepper. Serve immediately.

NUTRIENT ANALYSIS FOR ONE SERVING

Calories 157	Carbohydrates 27 g	Total Fat 3 g
Protein 6 g	Fiber 4 g	Saturated Fat 0 g
Sodium 154 mg	Sugars 3 g	Monounsaturated Fat 1 g
Cholesterol 0 mg		Polyunsaturated Fat 0 g

SESAME BROCCOLI

CARB COUNT **5g**

DIABETIC EXCHANGES

| 0 starch | 0 fruit | 0 milk |
| 1 vegetable | 0 protein | ½ fat |

SERVES 4

Quick, easy, and pretty on the plate, this side dish pairs well with Asian dishes. Try it with Szechuan Pork Stir-Fry (page 76) or Teriyaki Scallops (page 60). Look for sesame seeds in your supermarket's spice rack or at a natural-food store.

Put the sesame seeds in a small, dry nonstick frying pan over medium-high heat. Cook, stirring often, until lightly toasted, 3–5 minutes. Set aside.

In a large pot fitted with a steamer basket, bring 1 inch of water to a boil. Add the broccoli, cover, and steam until the stalks are tender, 7–9 minutes. Transfer to a serving bowl. Toss with the soy sauce, sesame oil, and pepper. Garnish with the toasted sesame seeds. Serve immediately.

1 tablespoon sesame seeds

1 lb broccoli, trimmed and cut into stalks, or 12 oz precut fresh broccoli florets or frozen broccoli stalks

4 teaspoons low-sodium soy sauce

1 teaspoon dark sesame oil

¼ teaspoon freshly ground pepper

NUTRIENT ANALYSIS FOR ONE SERVING

Calories 46	**Carbohydrates** 5 g	**Total Fat** 3 g
Protein 3 g	**Fiber** 2 g	**Saturated Fat** 0 g
Sodium 197 mg	**Sugars** 1 g	**Monounsaturated Fat** 1 g
Cholesterol 0 mg		**Polyunsaturated Fat** 1 g

CAULIFLOWER GRATIN

DIABETIC EXCHANGES

½ starch	0 fruit	0 milk
1 vegetable	½ protein	½ fat

SERVES 4

Topped with seasoned bread crumbs, this gratin, or French-style casserole, is an elegant dish suitable for company, yet it is easy to make. The cauliflower is coated with a low-fat cheese sauce, then the dish is baked until browned and bubbly.

Preheat the oven to 400°F.

In a large pot fitted with a steamer basket, bring 1 inch of water to a boil. Add the cauliflower, cover, and steam until tender, 7–8 minutes. Drain and keep warm.

In a saucepan over medium heat, combine the flour, milk, and nutmeg and whisk to blend. Cook until thickened, stirring frequently at first and then constantly as the sauce begins to thicken, 8–10 minutes. Remove from the heat and stir in the cheese, chives, and pepper.

Lightly coat the bottom and sides of a 1½-qt gratin dish or shallow baking dish with ½ teaspoon of the olive oil. Spoon the cauliflower into the dish, then pour the cheese sauce over.

Place the bread in a small food processor or blender and pulse to form coarse crumbs. Add the parsley and the remaining 1½ teaspoons olive oil and pulse to blend. Sprinkle the bread crumb mixture evenly over the cauliflower–cheese sauce mixture. Bake until the mixture is bubbly and the bread crumbs are lightly browned, about 15 minutes. Serve immediately.

5 cups cauliflower florets

3 tablespoons all-purpose flour

1⅓ cups nonfat milk

⅛ teaspoon freshly grated nutmeg

⅓ cup shredded fontina cheese

1 tablespoon chopped fresh chives

⅛ teaspoon freshly ground pepper

2 teaspoons olive oil

2 slices whole-wheat or multigrain bread, 1 oz each, torn into large pieces

1 tablespoon chopped fresh parsley

NUTRIENT ANALYSIS FOR ONE SERVING

Calories 109	**Carbohydrates** 13 g	**Total Fat** 4 g
Protein 6 g	**Fiber** 3 g	**Saturated Fat** 1 g
Sodium 144 mg	**Sugars** 5 g	**Monounsaturated Fat** 1 g
Cholesterol 7 mg		**Polyunsaturated Fat** 0 g

16g

SOYBEAN SUCCOTASH

SERVES 4

1 cup fresh or thawed frozen soybeans

1 small yellow crookneck squash, about 4 oz, coarsely chopped

1 strip center-cut bacon

½ small white or yellow onion, chopped

1 cup fresh corn kernels, cut from 1 ear of corn

2 tablespoons chopped fresh parsley

¼ teaspoon salt

⅛ teaspoon freshly ground pepper

Fresh soybeans, also called edamame, taste a bit like fresh English peas and make a pleasing stand-in for lima beans in this mix of beans, corn, and squash. Serve with Pork Loin with Apples (page 74) or Cornmeal-Crusted Snapper Fillets (page 57).

In a small pot fitted with a steamer basket, bring 1 inch of water to a boil. Add the soybeans and squash, cover, and steam until nearly tender, 5–6 minutes. Remove from the heat, drain, and set aside.

In a large nonstick frying pan, cook the bacon over medium heat until lightly browned, 2–3 minutes. Transfer the bacon to a paper towel to drain.

With a clean paper towel, wipe the frying pan. Add the onion and corn to the pan and sauté over medium heat until tender, about 5 minutes. Add the soybean mixture and continue cooking until the vegetables are warmed through, 2–3 minutes longer. Remove from the heat. Chop the bacon and stir into the soybean mixture along with the parsley, salt, and pepper. Serve immediately.

NUTRIENT ANALYSIS FOR ONE SERVING

Calories 113	Carbohydrates 16 g	Total Fat 4 g
Protein 7 g	Fiber 4 g	Saturated Fat 1 g
Sodium 193 mg	Sugars 1 g	Monounsaturated Fat 1 g
Cholesterol 2 mg		Polyunsaturated Fat 2 g

POLENTA WITH GARLIC & BASIL

SERVES 6

1 teaspoon olive oil

2 large cloves garlic, minced

3 cups fat-free, no-salt-added chicken broth

1 cup water

1 cup coarse polenta

⅛ teaspoon salt

¼ cup chopped fresh basil

¼ cup grated Parmesan cheese

A coarse grind of cornmeal cooked simply in broth, polenta is delicious with fresh basil and Parmesan cheese. For the best flavor, use freshly grated Parmigiano-Reggiano from Italy. Leftovers can be cut into wedges and grilled or pan seared.

In a saucepan, heat the olive oil over medium-high heat. Add the garlic and sauté until soft and fragrant, about 2 minutes. Add the broth and water. Gradually add the polenta, whisking constantly to avoid lumps. Bring the mixture to a boil, whisking frequently. Reduce the heat to low and simmer uncovered, whisking frequently, until the mixture is very thick, 15–20 minutes. Remove from the heat, stir in the salt, basil, and cheese, and serve.

NUTRIENT ANALYSIS FOR ONE SERVING

Calories 145	Carbohydrates 25 g	Total Fat 2 g
Protein 7 g	Fiber 3 g	Saturated Fat 1 g
Sodium 196 mg	Sugars 0 g	Monounsaturated Fat 1 g
Cholesterol 3 mg		Polyunsaturated Fat 0 g

8g

SAUTÉED WINTER GREENS

SERVES 4

1 bunch kale, ½ lb, about 14 large leaves

1 bunch collard greens, ½ lb, about 6 large leaves

1 bunch red or green Swiss chard, ½ lb, about 8 large leaves

1½ teaspoons olive oil

3 cloves garlic, minced

⅛ teaspoon salt

⅛ teaspoon freshly ground pepper

1 tablespoon balsamic or red wine vinegar

Don't be surprised by the amount of chopped kale, collards, and Swiss chard in this recipe—fresh greens cook down greatly. All it takes to finish this quick and tasty dish is a sprinkling of salt and pepper and a splash of mildly sweet balsamic vinegar.

Remove the tough stems and ribs of the kale and discard. Coarsely chop the kale greens and set them aside. Remove the tough stems and ribs of the collard greens and Swiss chard and discard. Coarsely chop the collard greens and then chard greens, keeping them separate from each other and from the chopped kale.

In a large pot fitted with a steamer basket, bring 1 inch of water to a boil. Spread the kale in a single layer on the bottom; top with the collard greens and then the chard. Cover and steam until the greens are tender, about 10 minutes. Drain and set aside.

In a large nonstick frying pan, heat the olive oil over medium heat. Stir in the garlic and sauté until it just begins to brown, 45–60 seconds. Add the steamed greens and sauté until the liquid is completely evaporated. Remove from the heat and stir in the salt, pepper, and vinegar. Serve immediately.

NUTRIENT ANALYSIS FOR ONE SERVING

Calories 55	Carbohydrates 8 g	Total Fat 2 g
Protein 3 g	Fiber 3 g	Saturated Fat 0 g
Sodium 200 mg	Sugars 2 g	Monounsaturated Fat 1 g
Cholesterol 0 mg		Polyunsaturated Fat 0 g

MASHED SWEET POTATOES

SERVES 4

Sweet potatoes—with all the comfort-food qualities of regular potatoes plus a dose of healthful beta-carotene—deserve to find their way into more dinners. Sprinkled with toasted pecans, these seasoned potatoes pair perfectly with roasted chicken.

Place the sweet potatoes in a saucepan and add water to cover the potatoes. Cover and bring to a boil over high heat. Reduce the heat to low and simmer until the potatoes are tender, 12–14 minutes.

While the sweet potatoes are cooking, put the pecans in a small, dry nonstick frying pan over medium-high heat. Cook, stirring often, until lightly toasted, 3–5 minutes. Set aside.

Drain the potatoes in a colander, then return them to the same saucepan over low heat. Add the broth, salt, and nutmeg. Using a potato masher or handheld blender, mash the potatoes until light and fluffy. Transfer to individual plates and top with the toasted pecans.

1 lb sweet potatoes, peeled and cut into ¾-inch chunks

2 tablespoons chopped pecans

⅓ cup fat-free, no-salt-added chicken or vegetable broth

¼ teaspoon salt

⅛ teaspoon freshly grated nutmeg

NUTRIENT ANALYSIS FOR ONE SERVING

Calories 121	**Carbohydrates** 22 g	**Total Fat** 3 g
Protein 2 g	**Fiber** 2 g	**Saturated Fat** 0 g
Sodium 171 mg	**Sugars** 10 g	**Monounsaturated Fat** 2 g
Cholesterol 0 mg		**Polyunsaturated Fat** 1 g

COUSCOUS WITH RAISINS & SPICES

CARB COUNT 28g

DIABETIC EXCHANGES

| 1½ starch | 0 fruit | 0 milk |
| ½ vegetable | ½ protein | 0 fat |

SERVES 6

Made like pasta from the hard durum wheat called semolina, couscous is a mild, easy-to-use grain product that cooks in minutes. Vegetables and seasonings now common in supermarkets give this dish its enticing North African flavor.

In a saucepan, heat the olive oil over medium heat. Add the onion, carrot, and garlic and sauté until fragrant, about 5 minutes. Add the coriander, cumin, and cinnamon to the vegetables and continue to sauté until blended, about 1 minute. Add the broth, raisins, and salt and bring to a simmer. Reduce the heat to low and simmer, uncovered, until the vegetables are tender, about 3 minutes. Stir in the couscous. Cover the saucepan and remove it from the heat. Let stand until the couscous has absorbed the liquid, about 5 minutes. Transfer to individual plates and top with the cilantro.

1 teaspoon olive oil

½ cup chopped yellow onion

1 small carrot, thinly sliced

3 cloves garlic, minced

1 teaspoon ground coriander

¾ teaspoon ground cumin

¼ teaspoon ground cinnamon

1¾ cups fat-free, no-salt-added chicken or vegetable broth

3 tablespoons dark raisins or golden raisins

¼ teaspoon salt

1 cup couscous or whole-wheat couscous

¼ cup chopped fresh cilantro

NUTRIENT ANALYSIS FOR ONE SERVING

Calories 149	**Carbohydrates** 28 g	**Total Fat** 1 g
Protein 6 g	**Fiber** 3 g	**Saturated Fat** 0 g
Sodium 156 mg	**Sugars** 5 g	**Monounsaturated Fat** 1 g
Cholesterol 0 mg		**Polyunsaturated Fat** 0 g

GRILLED SUMMER VEGETABLES

SERVES 4

This colorful dish takes full advantage of summer's bounty of squash, peppers, and eggplants. Brushed with vinaigrette and grilled, the vegetables take on a pleasing smokiness that makes them a fine accompaniment for grilled chicken or salmon.

Prepare a fire in a charcoal grill or preheat a gas grill or broiler. Position the cooking rack 4–6 inches from the heat source.

In a small bowl, combine the broth, vinegar, olive oil, garlic, salt, and pepper. Brush half of the broth mixture over the eggplants, bell peppers, squash, and onion. Place the vegetables on the grill rack or broiler pan. Grill or broil until the vegetables begin to brown, about 6 minutes. Turn the vegetables over and brush with the remaining broth mixture. Continue cooking until the vegetables are lightly browned and tender-crisp, about 5 minutes longer. Transfer to a platter and top with the basil.

¼ cup fat-free, no-salt-added chicken or vegetable broth

1 tablespoon balsamic vinegar

2 teaspoons olive oil

2 cloves garlic, minced

¼ teaspoon salt

¼ teaspoon freshly ground pepper

2 Asian eggplants, halved lengthwise

2 red or yellow bell peppers, or 1 of each, cut lengthwise into quarters and seeded

2 zucchini or yellow crookneck squash, or 1 of each, halved lengthwise

1 small red onion, cut into slices ¼ inch thick

2 tablespoons chopped fresh basil or chives

NUTRIENT ANALYSIS FOR ONE SERVING

Calories 88	Carbohydrates 15 g	Total Fat 3 g
Protein 4 g	Fiber 5 g	Saturated Fat 0 g
Sodium 165 mg	Sugars 8 g	Monounsaturated Fat 2 g
Cholesterol 0 mg		Polyunsaturated Fat 0 g

GREEN BEANS WITH TOMATOES & GARLIC

SERVES 4

- 1 lb green beans
- ½ cup coarsely chopped, seeded tomato
- 1 tablespoon capers, rinsed
- 1½ teaspoons olive oil
- 1 clove garlic, minced
- ⅛ teaspoon salt
- 1 anchovy fillet, mashed, or ½ teaspoon anchovy paste (optional)

The sweetness of green beans melds wonderfully with the traditional French blend of tomatoes, olive oil, garlic, and capers. To make this dish even more authentic, use delicate, thin French green beans.

Place the green beans in a frying pan or saucepan and add water to cover. Bring to a boil over high heat. Reduce the heat to low and simmer, uncovered, until tender, 4–6 minutes, depending on the beans' thickness. Drain.

While the beans are cooking, in a bowl, combine the tomato, capers, olive oil, garlic, and salt and stir to mix. Stir in the anchovy, if using.

Transfer the cooked beans to a serving bowl, add the tomato mixture, and toss to mix. Serve immediately.

NUTRIENT ANALYSIS FOR ONE SERVING

Calories 55	**Carbohydrates** 8 g	**Total Fat** 2 g
Protein 1 g	**Fiber** 4 g	**Saturated Fat** 0 g
Sodium 139 mg	**Sugars** 3 g	**Monounsaturated Fat** 1 g
Cholesterol 0 mg		**Polyunsaturated Fat** 0 g

ROASTED WINTER VEGETABLES

SERVES 4

CARB COUNT 14g

DIABETIC EXCHANGES
0 starch	0 fruit	0 milk
2½ vegetable	0 protein	½ fat

It's now easy to find once-exotic items such as fennel bulbs. The feathery tops resemble fresh dill and can be used like any fresh herb. Similar in texture to celery, fennel bulb has a subtle anise flavor that goes well in this mix of roasted vegetables.

Preheat the oven to 375°F.

Trim the ends of the fennel bulb and cut the bulb through the core into ¼-inch slices. Cut each brussels sprout through the core into halves. Combine the fennel, brussels sprouts, and carrots in a shallow roasting pan or rimmed baking sheet. Sprinkle the vegetables with the olive oil, salt, and pepper and toss to coat. Roast until the vegetables are tender, about 30 minutes. Sprinkle the vegetables with the chopped fennel fronds and the thyme, if desired.

1 large fennel bulb, about ½ lb, green fronds reserved for garnish (about 2 tablespoons chopped)

½ lb brussels sprouts

½ lb baby carrots

2 teaspoons olive oil

⅛ teaspoon salt

¼ teaspoon freshly ground pepper

1 tablespoon chopped fresh thyme (optional)

NUTRIENT ANALYSIS FOR ONE SERVING

Calories 82	**Carbohydrates** 14 g	**Total Fat** 3 g
Protein 3 g	**Fiber** 5 g	**Saturated Fat** 0 g
Sodium 136 mg	**Sugars** 4 g	**Monounsaturated Fat** 2 g
Cholesterol 0 mg		**Polyunsaturated Fat** 0 g

DESSERTS & SNACKS

Roasted Plums, 120

APPLE CRISP

SERVES 5

¼ cup unsweetened apple juice

2 teaspoons cornstarch

6 McIntosh or Jonathan apples, peeled, cored, and sliced (about 5 cups)

1 tablespoon almond-flavored liqueur, such as amaretto (optional)

1½ teaspoons ground cinnamon

⅓ cup old-fashioned rolled oats

1 tablespoon canola oil

¼ cup firmly packed light brown sugar

2 tablespoons chopped walnuts

This quick fruit crisp, made with walnuts and a small amount of healthful canola oil, is every bit as richly satisfying as apple pie, without any of the unhealthy saturated and trans fats.

Preheat the oven to 375°F.

In a bowl, combine the apple juice and cornstarch and stir until the cornstarch dissolves. Add the apples, the liqueur (if using), and 1 teaspoon of the cinnamon and toss well to mix. Transfer the mixture to an 8-inch square baking dish or a deep 9-inch pie dish.

In a bowl, combine the oats and canola oil and mix well. Add the brown sugar, walnuts, and the remaining ½ teaspoon cinnamon. Sprinkle the mixture over the apples. Bake until the apples are tender and the topping is golden brown, 35–40 minutes. Serve warm or at room temperature.

NUTRIENT ANALYSIS FOR ONE SERVING

Calories 180	Carbohydrates 34 g	Total Fat 6 g
Protein 1 g	Fiber 3 g	Saturated Fat 0 g
Sodium 6 mg	Sugars 26 g	Monounsaturated Fat 2 g
Cholesterol 0 mg		Polyunsaturated Fat 2 g

ROASTED PLUMS

SERVES 4

2 tablespoons frozen apple juice concentrate, thawed

⅛ teaspoon ground cinnamon

Pinch of freshly grated nutmeg

6 plums, about 1 lb total weight, cut in half and pitted

1 teaspoon canola oil

4 teaspoons cream sherry (optional)

2 teaspoons chopped pistachios

Both sweet and tart by nature, plums are the ideal fruit for this flavorful dessert. Peaches and apricots also lend themselves wonderfully to this preparation, which is reminiscent of baked apples. Top with vanilla yogurt instead of sherry, if you prefer.

Preheat the oven to 450°F.

In a bowl, combine the apple juice concentrate, cinnamon, and a generous pinch of nutmeg. Add the plums and toss gently to mix.

Lightly coat the bottom of a small baking dish with the canola oil. Arrange the plum halves cut sides down in a single layer in the dish. Pour in any of the juice mixture remaining in the bowl. Bake until the plums are tender and the juice has reduced to a syrup, about 15 minutes. Drizzle each serving with 1 teaspoon sherry, if desired, and sprinkle with the pistachios. Serve immediately, or let cool to room temperature and serve.

NUTRIENT ANALYSIS FOR ONE SERVING

Calories 101	**Carbohydrates** 18 g	**Total Fat** 3 g
Protein 1 g	**Fiber** 2 g	**Saturated Fat** 0 g
Sodium 2 mg	**Sugars** 10 g	**Monounsaturated Fat** 2 g
Cholesterol 0 mg		**Polyunsaturated Fat** 1 g

PISTACHIO CLOUDS

MAKES 24 COOKIES

CARB COUNT

8g

DIABETIC EXCHANGES

0 starch   0 fruit   ½ other carbs
0 vegetable   0 protein   0 fat

Roasted pistachios and cocoa powder give these crisp cookies a delightfully rich flavor, while rolled oats add some fiber and egg whites keep them feather light. What's more, they're a breeze to make. Serve for dessert or as a midafternoon snack.

Preheat the oven to 325°F.

In a bowl, combine the oats, brown sugar, cocoa powder, pistachios, flour, and salt and stir to mix well. Set aside.

In a spotlessly clean, large bowl or the bowl of a stand mixer, beat the egg whites at high speed until soft peaks form. Add the granulated sugar, 1 tablespoon at a time, and the vanilla, beating until stiff peaks form. Gently fold the oat mixture into the beaten egg whites, mixing just until no white streaks remain.

Lightly coat 2 baking sheets with cooking spray. With a soup spoon, drop the dough onto the baking sheets in rounded spoonfuls, about 1½ tablespoons each, spaced 1 inch apart. Bake until set, 16–18 minutes. Let the cookies cool on the baking sheets for 1 minute. With a spatula, transfer the cookies to cooling racks and let cool completely. Store tightly covered at room temperature for up to 2 days or freeze for up to 2 weeks.

¾ cup quick-cooking rolled oats

⅓ cup firmly packed light brown sugar

⅓ cup unsweetened cocoa powder

⅓ cup chopped toasted pistachios or pecans (page 138)

2 tablespoons all-purpose flour

¼ teaspoon salt

4 egg whites

¼ cup granulated sugar

1 teaspoon vanilla extract

Cooking spray

NUTRIENT ANALYSIS FOR ONE COOKIE

Calories 47	**Carbohydrates** 8 g	**Total Fat** 1 g
Protein 2 g	**Fiber** 1 g	**Saturated Fat** 0 g
Sodium 35 mg	**Sugars** 5 g	**Monounsaturated Fat** 1 g
Cholesterol 0 mg		**Polyunsaturated Fat** 0 g

MIXED BERRY SUMMER PUDDING

CARB COUNT 41g

DIABETIC EXCHANGES

1 starch	1 fruit	0 milk
0 vegetable	0 protein	0 fat

SERVES 4

This venerable English dessert may by tradition be called a pudding, but it's really something simpler and better: tangy ripe berries sandwiched in juice-sweetened bread, then refrigerated until the ingredients gel.

In a small saucepan, combine the blueberries, blackberries, raspberries, grape juice concentrate, orange zest, and orange juice. Bring the mixture to a boil over medium-high heat. Cook at a gentle boil for 2 minutes. Remove from the heat and stir in the preserves. Set aside.

Using a ½-cup ramekin (round individual baking dish) as a guide, cut a round from 4 of the bread slices to fit into the bottom of each of 4 ramekins. Slice the bread scraps to fit the sides of the ramekins and tuck in to fit. Carefully spoon one-fourth of the berry mixture into each ramekin, reserving any extra juice. Cut the remaining 2 bread slices to make rounds that fit into the top of the ramekins. Discard the remaining bread scraps. Press the bread gently with your fingers so it absorbs the juice from the berries. Cover each ramekin with plastic wrap and refrigerate until ready to serve, up to 8 hours.

To serve, place a small dessert plate over the top of each ramekin, invert the plate and ramekin together, and shake gently to transfer the pudding to the plate. Top with the reserved juice and garnish with a mint leaf and blackberries. Serve immediately.

1 cup fresh blueberries or frozen blueberries, thawed

1 cup fresh blackberries or frozen blackberries, thawed, plus extra berries for garnish

1 cup fresh raspberries or frozen raspberries, thawed

2 tablespoons frozen unsweetened white grape juice concentrate, thawed

½ teaspoon grated orange zest

⅓ cup orange juice

2 tablespoons seedless all-fruit raspberry or blueberry preserves

6 thin slices firm, whole-grain bread, crusts removed

Fresh mint leaves for garnish

NUTRIENT ANALYSIS FOR ONE SERVING

Calories 191	**Carbohydrates** 41 g	**Total Fat** 2 g
Protein 5 g	**Fiber** 8 g	**Saturated Fat** 0 g
Sodium 199 mg	**Sugars** 19 g	**Monounsaturated Fat** 1 g
Cholesterol 0 mg		**Polyunsaturated Fat** 1 g

MANGO-LIME SORBET

SERVES 4

2 large mangoes, about 1½ lb total weight, peeled and coarsely chopped

¼ cup frozen unsweetened white grape juice concentrate, thawed

½ cup nonfat milk

1½ teaspoons grated lime zest

¼ cup fresh lime juice

Ripe mangoes are so sweet and flavorful they can be puréed into a sensational sorbet with just a touch of added sugar—or, as in this recipe, a dollop of unsweetened grape juice. Perfectly ripe mangoes are mildly fragrant and slightly soft to the touch.

In a food processor, combine the mangoes, grape juice concentrate, milk, lime zest, and lime juice and process until smooth. Pour the mango mixture into a glass measuring cup or bowl and chill in the refrigerator for at least 2 hours.

Pour the chilled mango mixture into an ice-cream maker and freeze according to the manufacturer's directions. Serve immediately, or spoon the sorbet into a freezer-safe container and freeze until ready to serve.

NUTRIENT ANALYSIS FOR ONE SERVING

Calories 86	**Carbohydrates** 21 g	**Total Fat** 0 g
Protein 1 g	**Fiber** 2 g	**Saturated Fat** 0 g
Sodium 19 mg	**Sugars** 19 g	**Monounsaturated Fat** 0 g
Cholesterol 0 mg		**Polyunsaturated Fat** 0 g

BALSAMIC-GLAZED BERRIES & TANGERINES

CARB COUNT 25g

DIABETIC EXCHANGES

| 0 starch | 1 fruit | ½ other carbs |
| 0 vegetable | 0 protein | ½ fat |

SERVES 4

This elegant and delicious dessert takes just minutes to prepare. For an alternate sauce, combine 2 tablespoons peach or apricot preserves (remove large fruit pieces) with 1 tablespoon white wine vinegar. Spoon over the fruit and sprinkle with almonds.

Cut the tangerine segments in half crosswise and combine them with the sliced strawberries in small individual bowls, dividing evenly. In a small saucepan over medium heat, combine the vinegar and brown sugar. Bring to a simmer, stirring frequently, and simmer, uncovered, for 1 minute. Remove the pan from the heat and let stand until the glaze thickens, 1–2 minutes. Spoon the glaze over the fruit and top with the almonds.

4 tangerines or clementines, peeled and separated into segments

2 cups sliced strawberries

2 tablespoons balsamic vinegar

2 tablespoons firmly packed light brown sugar

3 tablespoons sliced almonds

NUTRIENT ANALYSIS FOR ONE SERVING

Calories 125	Carbohydrates 25 g	Total Fat 3 g
Protein 2 g	Fiber 5 g	Saturated Fat 0 g
Sodium 6 mg	Sugars 21 g	Monounsaturated Fat 1 g
Cholesterol 0 mg		Polyunsaturated Fat 1 g

PINEAPPLE SMOOTHIE

SERVES 2

1 small banana, about 5 oz,
  cut into 1-inch chunks

1 tablespoon unsweetened dried
  coconut

1 cup fresh pineapple chunks,
  plus diced pineapple for garnish

½ cup nonfat plain yogurt

½ cup soy milk

¼ cup mango nectar or orange
  juice

2 tablespoons toasted wheat germ

⅛ teaspoon freshly grated nutmeg

The refreshing fruit blends called smoothies are among the simplest and most versatile of snacks. In this version, tangy pineapple and ripe banana complement the protein-rich yogurt and soy milk, while nutty wheat germ adds fiber and nutrients.

Place the banana chunks in a freezer-safe bag or container, transfer to the freezer, and freeze until firm, at least 3 hours.

Place the coconut in a small, dry frying pan over medium heat and cook, stirring constantly, until lightly toasted, about 2 minutes. Transfer to a plate and set aside.

In a food processor or blender, combine the frozen banana, pineapple chunks, and yogurt. Process until smooth. Add the soy milk, mango nectar, wheat germ, and nutmeg. Pulse to blend.

Pour the mixture into two 8-oz glasses. Garnish with the diced fresh pineapple and coconut. Serve immediately.

NUTRIENT ANALYSIS FOR ONE SERVING

Calories 197	**Carbohydrates** 38 g	**Total Fat** 3 g
Protein 8 g	**Fiber** 4 g	**Saturated Fat** 1 g
Sodium 63 mg	**Sugars** 28 g	**Monounsaturated Fat** 1 g
Cholesterol 1 mg		**Polyunsaturated Fat** 1 g

17g

OATMEAL COOKIES

MAKES 24 COOKIES

2 cups old-fashioned rolled oats

¾ cup all-purpose flour

1 teaspoon baking soda

1½ teaspoons ground cinnamon

¼ teaspoon salt

¼ teaspoon freshly grated nutmeg

½ cup golden raisins or dark raisins

½ cup granulated sugar

¼ cup canola oil

¼ cup unsweetened applesauce

¼ cup firmly packed light brown sugar

1 egg white

1 teaspoon vanilla extract

Moist, chewy, and aromatic with familiar spices, these foolproof cookies made with fiber-rich old-fashioned rolled oats easily qualify as a heart-healthy dessert or snack. For the very best flavor, use freshly grated nutmeg.

Preheat the oven to 350°F.

In a bowl, combine the oats, flour, baking soda, cinnamon, salt, and nutmeg. In a large bowl, combine the raisins, granulated sugar, canola oil, applesauce, brown sugar, egg white, and vanilla. Stir well to mix. Add the oat mixture to the raisin mixture and stir well to mix.

With a soup spoon, drop the dough onto 2 ungreased baking sheets in rounded spoonfuls, about 1½ tablespoons each, spaced 2 inches apart. Bake until the cookies are firm, 10–12 minutes. Let the cookies cool on the baking sheets for 2 minutes. With a spatula, transfer the cookies to wire cooling racks and let cool completely.

NUTRIENT ANALYSIS FOR ONE COOKIE

Calories 99	**Carbohydrates** 17 g	**Total Fat** 3 g
Protein 2 g	**Fiber** 1 g	**Saturated Fat** 0 g
Sodium 81 mg	**Sugars** 9 g	**Monounsaturated Fat** 2 g
Cholesterol 0 mg		**Polyunsaturated Fat** 1 g

BLUEBERRY BRAN MUFFINS

MAKES **12 MUFFINS**

¾ cup all-purpose flour

¾ cup whole-wheat flour

¾ cup wheat bran

3 tablespoons freshly ground flaxseed or flaxseed meal

1¼ teaspoons baking soda

⅛ teaspoon salt

¾ cup low-fat buttermilk

½ cup nonfat plain yogurt

2 large eggs, lightly beaten

½ cup sugar

3 tablespoons canola oil, plus 1 teaspoon

1 cup fresh blueberries or frozen blueberries, thawed

The nutty flavor of these supremely light muffins comes from a mix of whole-wheat flour, wheat bran, and ground flaxseed, which is rich in heart-healthy omega-3 fatty acids. Antioxidant-rich blueberries add a burst of sweetness.

Preheat the oven to 350°F.

In a large bowl, combine the all-purpose flour, whole-wheat flour, wheat bran, ground flaxseed, baking soda, and salt. Whisk to blend.

In another bowl, combine the buttermilk, yogurt, beaten eggs, sugar, and 3 tablespoons of the canola oil. Whisk until well blended. Pour the buttermilk mixture into the flour mixture and stir until just moistened. (Do not overmix the batter, or the muffins will be tough.) Fold in the blueberries.

Coat the cups of a 12-cup nonstick muffin pan with the remaining 1 teaspoon canola oil, or lightly coat the pan with cooking spray. Spoon the batter into the muffin cups, filling each about two-thirds full. Bake until a toothpick inserted into the center of a muffin comes out clean, 18–20 minutes. Cool in the pan on a wire rack for 10 minutes. Remove the muffins from the pan and serve immediately, or let cool on the rack.

NUTRIENT ANALYSIS FOR ONE MUFFIN

Calories 166	**Carbohydrates** 26 g	**Total Fat** 6 g
Protein 5 g	**Fiber** 4 g	**Saturated Fat** 1 g
Sodium 190 mg	**Sugars** 11 g	**Monounsaturated Fat** 3 g
Cholesterol 36 mg		**Polyunsaturated Fat** 2 g

SPICY PITA CHIPS

DIABETIC EXCHANGES

| 1 starch | 0 fruit | 0 milk |
| 0 vegetable | 0 protein | ½ fat |

SERVES 4

These fiber-rich snacks get an invigorating zing from a dusting of cayenne pepper. For less spicy chips, reduce the amount of cayenne pepper to ⅛ teaspoon. Enjoy the chips plain, or serve with the Vegetable Platter with Hummus Dip (page 34).

Preheat the oven to 400°F.

Using a small, sharp knife, split each pita into 2 rounds. Stack the 4 rounds and make 3 crosswise cuts to form 24 pita wedges.

On a baking sheet, arrange the pita wedges rough sides up. With a pastry brush, lightly coat each wedge with the oil. Sprinkle the wedges evenly with the thyme, cayenne, and cheese. Bake until crisp and golden brown, 8–10 minutes. Serve warm or at room temperature. Store tightly covered at room temperature for up to 2 days.

2 whole-wheat pitas, 6 inches in diameter

1½ teaspoons olive oil or canola oil

½ teaspoon dried thyme

¼ teaspoon cayenne pepper

2 tablespoons grated Romano cheese

NUTRIENT ANALYSIS FOR ONE SERVING

Calories 88	**Carbohydrates** 13 g	**Total Fat** 3 g
Protein 3 g	**Fiber** 2 g	**Saturated Fat** 1 g
Sodium 157 mg	**Sugars** 0 g	**Monounsaturated Fat** 2 g
Cholesterol 3 mg		**Polyunsaturated Fat** 0 g

INGREDIENTS & TECHNIQUES

AL DENTE

Italian for "to the tooth," *al dente* refers to the firm texture traditionally desired in boiled dried pasta. It should not be hard at the center, but it should offer slight resistance when bitten. The best way to determine when it has reached this stage is by tasting the pasta near the end of its cooking time. Depending on its shape, most dried pasta requires 8 to 12 minutes of boiling.

BULGUR WHEAT

A staple in the Middle East, bulgur comes from whole wheat kernels that have been partially steamed, dried, and then cracked. It's widely available in a range of granulations, from a coarse grain for pilaf to a fine grinding for tabbouleh. Commonly used in salads, soups, and fillings, bulgur requires only brief soaking in water or a few minutes of cooking to bring out its nutty flavor.

BRAISING

This technique involves searing over high heat, then simmering in a tightly covered pot. Browning and long cooking develop deep flavors, while low heat and moisture coax tougher cuts of meat into tenderness. Braising helps swell the starches in firm vegetables like carrots, winter squash, and sweet potatoes, and soften the tough fibers in dark greens such as kale and collards.

CAPERS

The flower buds of a spiny Mediterranean shrub, capers have a pleasantly pungent flavor. They lend a bright piquancy to a wide variety of sauces, salads, and dips. Although commonly available pickled in vinegar, capers that have been packed in salt retain the best flavor and texture. Briefly soak pickled capers or rinse salted ones in cold water to remove excess salt before using.

CHILES

A staple around the world, chiles—hot peppers—vary widely in shape, color, flavor, and heat levels. Most ripen from green to bright red, sweetening as they redden. Popular and versatile jalapeños register medium to hot. Poblanos are larger, slightly milder, and dark green to red-brown in color. Roast them first to bring out their smoky, earthy flavor and then add them to soups, stews, and sauces.

DICING VEGETABLES

Cutting vegetables into even cubes creates visual appeal and promotes even cooking. Dice tiny cubes of bell pepper for garnishing or large chunks of potatoes for long simmering. In most recipes, ½-inch cubes serve well. To dice, first cut vegetables into thick slices with a large knife. Stack the slices, cut long pieces, then cut the pieces crosswise into cubes.

COOKING DRIED BEANS

For the best texture, soak dried beans in water for at least 8 hours or overnight; drain and rinse. In a large pot, combine beans and water to cover by 2 inches. Bring the beans to a boil, cover partially, and simmer over low heat until tender, 40 to 50 minutes. Continue as directed in the recipe. Most varieties yield about 2½ to 3 cups cooked beans for every 1 cup dried.

FLAXSEED

These tiny seeds, varying in color from pale gold to brown, have a nutty flavor that blends well in baked goods or cereals. For the best flavor and nutrient value, grind whole flaxseed in a coffee grinder, food processor, or blender. Whole flaxseed can be stored indefinitely at room temperature, but once ground, it should be kept in an airtight container in the refrigerator.

LENTILS

A staple in the Middle East for 8,000 years, lentils are now available in dozens of types grown around the world. Varieties include the common brown lentil found in most supermarkets, dark green Le Puy lentils from France, yellow lentils from India, and the small red lentils of Egypt. Although always dried, they do not require presoaking and cook to tenderness in only 20 to 30 minutes.

OLIVE OIL

Essential to Mediterranean cuisine, olive oils can be bright green and peppery or mellow gold and slightly sweet. Extra-virgin olive oil, the highest quality grade, retains the most color and flavor, but it's best reserved for sauces and quick sautés, as it loses character at even moderate temperatures. Regular olive oil, lighter in flavor and color, holds up well to high-heat cooking such as grilling.

NUTMEG, WHOLE

Native to Indonesia, nutmeg has a warm, sweet-spicy flavor that marries well with spinach, fish, meat fillings, milk-based dishes, and many desserts. Because its aromatic oils dissipate quickly once the seed is ground, try to use whole nutmeg whenever possible. Although special nutmeg graters ensure the finest shavings, a fine-holed or Microplane grater also works well.

PEELING MANGOES

To peel and dice a ripe mango, stand the fruit on one of its narrow ends. Cut the mango off-center, just grazing one side of the pit. Repeat on the other side. Score the cut side of the two lobes in a grid without piercing the peel. Press the mango lobes inside out and slice off the cubes of fruit near the peel. Finally, remove the peel from the fruit around the pit, then cut the fruit away from the pit.

PINE NUTS

Also known as pignoli or piñon nuts, these pale, slender nuts are laboriously harvested from the cones of pine trees indigenous to southern Europe and the southern United States. Ground or whole, raw or toasted, they lend richness to a wide variety of savory and sweet dishes, from classic Italian pesto and Mexican sweets to simple salads and pastas. They're especially good toasted.

SHALLOTS

Diminutive members of the onion family, shallots grow in small clusters much like garlic. Their papery, reddish brown skin covers white flesh tinged with pink or purple. Although layered like onions, with a similar pungent aroma, they are valued for their more delicate flavor, which is particularly good in sauces and vinaigrettes. Store shallots in a cool, dark place with good air circulation.

SESAME OIL

Made from toasted sesame seeds, dark sesame oil has a rich amber color and an intense, nutty flavor. Clear, refined sesame oils are better for high-heat cooking, but dark oils offer more flavor, even in tiny amounts. Look for them in Asian markets or the ethnic or international aisle of supermarkets. More perishable than other oils, dark sesame oil is best stored in the refrigerator.

SOYBEANS, FRESH

Also known as edamame, soybeans picked still in their pods retain a bright green color and a fresh, nutty flavor. Left whole, they can be boiled or steamed for a snack. Shelled, they're enjoyed like English peas in vegetable dishes, soups, or purées. Look for soybeans during summer in produce markets or year-round in the freezers of natural-food stores, Asian markets, and many large supermarkets.

SPECIALTY VINEGARS

French for "sour wine," vinegar forms when bacteria turn a fermented liquid into a weak solution of acetic acid. Red wine, white wine, balsamic, and sherry vinegars are among the best for cooking, as they display traits of the wines from which they are made, along with a sourness that makes them valuable in balancing flavors. Look for top-quality, unfiltered aged vinegars.

SWEET POTATOES

Although often confused with yams, sweet potatoes have a sweeter flavor and less starchy flesh. They are excellent baked whole, roasted or braised with a honey or maple syrup glaze, or mashed with a touch of cinnamon or nutmeg. Shop for sweet potatoes free of dark blemishes. Store in a cool, dark, well-ventilated place but avoid refrigerating them, as cold temperatures will alter their flavor.

SWEET ONIONS

The best-known varieties of these onions include Vidalia, Walla Walla, and Maui, named for regions in the United States where special soil and climate conditions allow the onions to develop a sweet flavor. Because they contain more moisture and sugar than regular onions, sweet onions bruise easily and so should be handled carefully. Store them in a cool, well-ventilated place.

TOASTING NUTS

Cooking nuts until they are golden deepens their flavor and improves their texture. You can toast nuts by baking them on a cookie sheet in a 325°F oven or by stirring them in a small, dry, nonstick frying pan over medium-high heat. Cook them just until they're fragrant and golden in color, about 10 minutes. Take care not to overcook them, as they will become bitter when scorched.

TOFU

Soy milk, made from cooked soybeans, forms tofu when curdled and pressed into blocks. Although bland, plain tofu readily absorbs flavors from marinades and sauces. The smooth texture of silken tofu is ideal for soups and for puréeing. Firm tofu, denser and coarser in texture, holds together well for stir-frying and grilling. To store tofu, submerge it in cold water and refrigerate.

WHEAT BRAN AND WHEAT GERM

During the milling of wheat, the kernel's outer covering, known as the bran, and its tiny embryo, the germ, are usually both removed. Sold in health-food stores and most supermarkets, wheat bran and wheat germ add nutrient value to cereals, casseroles, fillings, and baked goods. Unless the germ is defatted, it should be stored in an airtight container in the refrigerator.

VINAIGRETTE

Making a vinaigrette involves little more than whisking together a small amount of oil, vinegar, salt, pepper, and perhaps an aromatic ingredient such as garlic, shallots, a dab of prepared mustard, or some minced fresh herbs. In addition to dressing salads, a vinaigrette can be used as a marinade before roasting, a basting liquid at the grill, or a sauce for steamed vegetables.

ZEST

The thin outer peel of citrus fruits, known as the zest, is rich in aromatic oils. A fine-holed or Microplane grater will shred the zest into delicate shavings for marinades or rubs. Use a zester to create thin, elegant strips for garnish. Take care not to cut or grate into the white, pulpy pith that lies just beneath the outer peel, as it has a spongy texture and an unpleasantly bitter flavor.

INDEX

MEREDITH® BOOKS

Editor in Chief: Linda Raglan Cunningham

Publisher: James D. Blume
Executive Director, Marketing: Jeffrey Myers
Executive Director, New Business Development: Todd M. Davis
Executive Director, Sales: Ken Zagor
Director, Operations: George A. Susral
Director, Production: Douglas M. Johnston
Business Director: Jim Leonard

Vice President and General Manager: Douglas J. Guendel

Meredith Publishing Group
President, Publishing Group: Stephen M. Lacy
Vice President-Publishing Director: Bob Mate

Meredith Corporation
Chairman and Chief Executive Officer: William T. Kerr

In Memoriam: E.T. Meredith III (1933–2003)

AMERICAN MEDICAL ASSOCIATION

Executive Vice President,
   Chief Executive Officer: Michael D. Maves, M.D.
Senior Vice President,
   Publishing and Business Services: Robert A. Musacchio, Ph.D.
Vice President, Business Products: Anthony J. Frankos
Chief Operations Officer, AMA Press: Mary Lou White
Managing Editor: Donna Kotulak
Writer: Pam Brick
Editors: Robin Husayko, Steve Michaels
Copy Editor: Reuben Rios
Art Editor: Mary Ann Albanese
Medical Editor: Bonnie Chi-Lum, M.D., M.P.H.
Contributing Editor: Maryellen Westerberg, Dr.P.H., R.D., C.D.E.
Consultants: Clair M. Callan, M.D., Thomas Houston, M.D.

The recommendations and information in this book are appropriate
in most cases and current as of the date of publication. For specific
information, concerning your or a family member's medical
condition, the AMA suggests that you consult a physician.

WELDON OWEN INC.

Chief Executive Officer: John Owen
President and Chief Operating Officer: Terry Newell
Vice President International Sales: Stuart Laurence
Creative Director: Gaye Allen
Associate Creative Director: Leslie Harrington
Associate Publisher: Val Cipollone
Managing Editor: Sheridan Warrick
Designer: Leon Yu
Editorial Assistants: Mitch Goldman, Juli Vendzules
Copy Editor and Proofreader: Carrie Bradley and Desne Ahlers
Indexer: Ken DellaPenta
Production Director: Chris Hemesath
Color Specialist: Teri Bell
Production Coordinator: Todd Rechner

The American Medical Association Diabetes Cookbook
Conceived and produced by Weldon Owen Inc.
814 Montgomery Street, San Francisco, CA 94133
Telephone: 415-291-0100 Fax: 415-291-8841

Copyright © 2004 Weldon Owen Inc.
Introduction Copyright © 2004 American Medical Association
All rights reserved, including the right of reproduction in whole
or in part in any form.

First printed in 2004
10 9 8 7 6 5 4 3 2 1

ISBN: 0-696-22152-7
Printed by Midas Printing Limited, China

Acknowledgments
Thanks to Kyrie Forbes, Karin Skaggs, Joan Olson, and Robin Terra
for design assistance; Joseph De Leo for art direction; Suzette
Kaminsky, Kim Konecny, Erin Quon, and Dan Becker for food styling;
Joe Maer and Leigh Noë for prop styling; Kevin Kerr and Selena
Aument for assisting in the studio; and Heather Dunn, Gina Bessire,
Tanya Henry, and Jackie Mancuso for modeling.

Photographs by Sheri Giblin: pages 9 (bottom right), 13 (three at left),
14 (middle at right), 15, 16 (three at right), 25 (third from top), 26, 32,
44, 52, 55, 65, 79, 82, 85, 86, 89, 94, 110, 114, 116, 119.